CULTURES OF THE WORLD
Netherlands

Cavendish
Square
New York

Published in 2016 by Cavendish Square Publishing, LLC
243 5th Avenue, Suite 136, New York, NY 10016
Copyright © 2016 by Cavendish Square Publishing, LLC

Third Edition

Website: cavendishsq.com

This publication represents the opinions and views of the author based on his or her personal experience, knowledge, and research. The information in this book serves as a general guide only. The author and publisher have used their best efforts in preparing this book and disclaim liability rising directly or indirectly from the use and application of this book.

CPSIA Compliance Information: Batch #CW16CSQ

All websites were available and accurate when this book was sent to press.

Library of Congress Cataloging-in-Publication Data
Names: Seward, Pat, 1939- | Arora Lal, Sunandini. | Paley, Caitlyn.
Title: Netherlands / Pat Seward, Sunandini Arora Lal, and Caitlyn Paley.
Description: New York : Cavendish Square Pub., [2016] | Series: Cultures of the world | Includes bibliographical references and index. | Description based on print version record and CIP data provided by publisher; resource not viewed.
Identifiers: LCCN 2015045080 (print) | LCCN 2015041808 (ebook) | ISBN 9781502616968 (eBook) | ISBN 9781502616951 (library bound)
Subjects: LCSH: Netherlands--Juvenile literature.
Classification: LCC DJ18 (print) | LCC DJ18 .S49 2016 (ebook) | DDC 949.2--dc23
LC record available at http://lccn.loc.gov/2015045080

Writers: Pat Seward, Sunandini Arora Lal, and Caitlyn Paley
Editorial Director: David McNamara
Editor: Kristen Susienka
Copy Editor: Nathan Heidelberger
Art Director: Jeffrey Talbot
Designer: Alan Sliwinski
Senior Production Manager: Jennifer Ryder-Talbot
Production Editor: Renni Johnson
Photo Research: J8 Media

PICTURE CREDITS

Printed in the United States of America

CONTENTS

NETHERLANDS TODAY

THE HISTORY OF THE NETHERLANDS, MORE FORMALLY KNOWN as the Kingdom of the Netherlands (and sometimes also called Holland), stretches back to antiquity. Over 250,000 years ago, hunter-gatherers occupied the region. They lived in groups and survived off the land and animals around them. In 100 BCE, Romans settled an area now known as Maastricht. Today the Dutch people commemorate their rich heritage and honor famous citizens like Vincent Van Gogh and Anne Frank. The Netherlands is a country steeped in tradition. The Dutch still celebrate holidays that harken back to the founding of their monarchy. They eat foods that have been made for hundreds of years. Many ride bicycles as their primary means of transportation. In fact, bicycles outnumber cars three to one!

When people outside of the Netherlands think of the country, they picture Amsterdam, windmills, and wooden clogs. Yet the Netherlands is so much more. Against the idyllic backdrop of tulip fields, the Netherlands is a modern nation at the frontlines of art and architecture, geopolitics, and scientific discovery.

Today the Netherlands blends tradition with new approaches as the European continent endures rapid change brought by the uncertainties of harsh economic

"Cube houses" in Rotterdam are representative of the country's cutting-edge architecture.

decisions, political tension, a sharp increase in immigration, and the ever-present threat of terrorism. The Netherlands artfully combines the old with the new and evolves without losing sight of its strong sense of national identity.

BIG CHANGES

In 2013, after Queen Beatrix abdicated the throne, the Kingdom of the Netherlands inaugurated Willem-Alexander, their first king in over 100 years. Prior to Beatrix's abdication, queens had ruled for 123 years. The monarchy is the perfect representation of how the Dutch are rooted in the past without compromising their vision for the future. King Willem-Alexander reigns over the nation, which is a republic with a constitutional monarchy. The Dutch people elect a prime minister who works alongside the king and parliament to govern the country. This unique blend of the monarchy and democracy shows how the Dutch honor their traditions and adapt to a changing world.

The shift from queens to a king isn't the only big change the nation has faced in recent years. The population is changing thanks to an influx of immigrants in record-breaking numbers. This increase led to the enactment of sweeping immigration reform in 2013. The Modern Migration Policy Act and National Visa Act require immigrants to have a sponsor in the Netherlands and make illegal residence a crime. New citizens with different customs and perspectives have also caused the Netherlands to consider banning burqas in public places, like schools and hospitals, due to security concerns.

ECONOMIC SHIFTS

The economy is another focal point in the Netherlands today. The nation is slowly rebuilding their economy after a two-year recession spanning from 2012 to 2014. The recession saw a spike in unemployment and a drop in consumer spending. This was an unusual occurrence for the robust economy that the Netherlands has historically enjoyed. The Netherlands' economy has always been one of the strongest in the world. The World Bank ranks the country as a "high income" nation. The Netherlands' gross domestic product is $869.5 billion. This figure earned the Netherlands the seventeenth spot on the list of the world's biggest economies according to the World Bank.

The Dutch attribute their strong gross domestic product (GDP) to their exports. According to the Netherlands Enterprise Agency, 86.7 percent of the nation's GDP is the result of exporting goods and services. The Dutch produce agricultural products, fuels, machinery, and consumer goods for nations around the world. Signs like a recovering housing market point to a strengthening economy, but the citizens of the Netherlands are still feeling

King Willem-Alexander's inauguration on April 30, 2013, was an historic day.

Prime Minister Mark Rutte is a member of the People's Party for Freedom and Democracy.

the effects of the recession. Furthermore, the economic crisis in Greece, another member of the European Union like the Netherlands, has widespread consequences. These consequences are financial and political. The Dutch prime minister Mark Rutte's vote to provide Greece with a third bailout in 2015 conflicts with his campaign promise that the Netherlands would not send any more financial assistance to the insolvent country. Rutte's decision resulted in politicians at the opposite end of the ideological spectrum, namely Party for Freedom leader Geert Wilders, to say that Rutte misled voters.

CHANGING LAWS

Aside from museums and the famous canals, the Netherlands' capital city, Amsterdam, has long been famous for its lenient laws. Tourists come from around the world to find "soft drugs" in coffee shops. However, in 2011, the Netherlands began to crack down on the buying and selling of these drugs, especially marijuana. The government was concerned about illegal drug trafficking across international borders. For a nation that has been known as liberal, this marked the beginning of a cultural shift. However, the Netherlands is still liberal about social issues. The nation was the first to legalize same-sex marriage, also granting same-sex couples adoption rights. The Netherlands is also exploring the expansion of legal euthanasia for terminally ill children under the age of twelve.

LOOKING FORWARD

The Netherlands is a rare combination of progressive and conservative. It is a nation of artists, scientists, politicians, farmers, and big thinkers. While the country is changing rapidly in the twenty-first century, the Dutch have maintained a rich culture. Traditional Dutch festivals, music, and art forms are alive and well. The strong heritage of the Netherlands attracts millions of tourists every year.

Old traditions and contemporary culture meet at a cheese market.

Tourism is a driving force in the Dutch economy. As Europe navigates the changes that immigration, economic disaster, and war have brought, the Netherlands stands at the forefront, ready to tackle new challenges without compromising Dutch identity.

GEOGRAPHY

Amsterdam is known for its picturesque canals, which draw tourists from all over.

1

T HE DUTCH IDENTITY IS inextricably tied to the country's geography. The Netherlands, which borders Germany and Belgium, has a population of nearly 17 million people. These 16.8 million Dutch citizens live on under 17,000 square miles (44,030 square kilometers) of habitable land. With so little space, the Dutch have invented creative solutions, including reclaiming land that was once underwater. Another creative solution is harnessing wind power— the nation is known for its windmills.

The history and economy of the Dutch people have been strongly influenced by their continuous battle with the sea and the rivers that flow through their low-lying land.

While for many, "the Netherlands" brings Amsterdam to mind, the country has twelve provinces and many other vibrant cities.

REGIONS AND PROVINCES

Much of the Netherlands consists of land reclaimed from the sea over the past seven or eight hundred years. About one-third of the total area lies below sea level, with the lowest point, near Rotterdam, 22 feet (6.7 meters) below sea level. More than half the country is less than 16 feet (4.9 m) above sea level, and because of the presence of large lakes such as the IJsselmeer (EH-sul-meer), one-sixth of the country is underwater.

This map shows the Netherlands' distinct provinces.

The low-lying western coastal region is characterized by polders, dikes, canals, and lakes. A polder is an area of reclaimed land, often below sea level, inside a dike or wall constructed to keep the sea from flooding in. Polders can span many square miles and often contain towns and villages, in addition to large expanses of farmland. Many Dutch cities, including Amsterdam and The Hague, are built on polders.

Most of the lakes are found in the polder region. The Netherlands' largest lake is the IJsselmeer. In 1932, the Dutch dammed the Zuiderzee (ZOU-der-zay), originally an inlet of the North Sea. A 19-mile (30-kilometer) barrier dam was built, linking the provinces of North Holland and Friesland (FREES-land). Over the years, the resulting lake, the IJsselmeer, has become freshwater because of the continuous freshwater flow from the IJssel River. Friesland—a farming province with its own distinct language—lies to the north of the IJsselmeer. The southern part of the lake has been reclaimed to form a new province called Flevoland (FLAY-voh-land).

Over many centuries, sand deposited by the sea has built up dunes along the coastline, resulting in the string of low-lying Frisian Islands. These enclose the Waddenzee (WAH-den-zay)—another inlet of the North Sea—and protect the coast from flooding. The waters here are seldom more than 10 feet (3 m) deep even at high tide, and it is possible to walk from the mainland to the islands across the mud flats at low tide.

Along the southwest coast, the Schelde (SGHEL-duh), Waal, and Maas Rivers form a complex river delta. This delta province, Zeeland (meaning "land of the sea"), has always been vulnerable to flooding.

The inner parts of the country are at higher altitudes than the polder region, so they are not threatened by flooding, but these provinces are not as well irrigated by rivers. Inland areas, such as the Limburg Province and the region along the German border, have poor soil and low hills. The highest point, Vaalserberg, at 1,053 feet (321 m), is in the far southeast where the Dutch, German, and Belgian borders meet.

THE POWER IN THE WIND

Were it not for the windmill, the Netherlands as we know it would not exist today. For more than six hundred years, the Dutch have used windmills to drain their land and keep it dry. Wherever one looks, there are windmills of one kind or another: small meadow mills in the fields, mills standing on artificial hills, mills with external stages or balconies, brick mills, wooden mills, and thatched mills. It is almost impossible to travel any significant distance without seeing either the chunky traditional mill with its broad sails or its modern descendant—the tall wind turbine with its shining blades spinning in the breeze.

The Frisian Islands extend through Denmark and Germany; the Netherlands' portion is sometimes called the West Frisian Islands.

Although they were primarily used for drainage during their height of popularity, windmills also performed many other tasks. Initially they were developed for grinding grain such as wheat and corn, then spices, paint, and flint for pottery. In 1594, Cornelis Corneliszoon van Uitgeest built the first wind-powered sawmill. Other types of mills were developed for creating wood pulp used for paper, for the extraction of linseed and rapeseed oil, and for pounding hemp.

The earliest mills were post mills, in which all the moving parts—the sails, the gearing, and the millstones—were contained in a hut-like structure that turned on a central vertical post. Interior wooden gears turned the sails. Access to the cramped interior was by means of a short ladder at the rear of the mill. Generally, post mills and their close relatives, the wip mills—with their rectangular mill houses and pyramid-shaped bases—were quite small. Their size tended to limit their uses to grinding corn and pumping water. Nevertheless, they were constructed in the hundreds, and they can still be seen in significant numbers today.

Since windmills were such a visible and important part of the landscape, they were also used for sending messages. Sails that were set at vertical or horizontal meant that the mill was ready to start work. If the sails were at

Windmills are widely photographed today, but centuries ago they were memorialized in paint by famous artists like Rembrandt.

45 degrees to the ground, the windmill could not work. News of a birth was signaled by the vertical sails being stopped just before reaching the highest point; deaths were signaled by sails stopped just after the highest point. On special occasions, the sails were decorated with baskets, tin hearts, garlands of flowers, and angels.

Windmills have their own names, which can be seen painted on the head, just below the point where the sails are attached. A visitor might see "Goliath," with "The Four Winds" and "de Jonge Hendrik" a little farther on. The parchment on which the 1776 Declaration of Independence was written came from a windmill called "Dee Schoolmeester." The English word "gang" is said to come from a Dutch word meaning a group of windmills working together.

At one time, the Netherlands could boast between nine and ten thousand active windmills, but their small capacity, their vulnerability to fire and wind damage, and the increasing availability of better sources of power meant that they could not survive. By the end of World War I, the windmill as a serious source of industrial power had ended. In recent times, their function has been taken over by the electric motor and the electric pump. It seems the days when the windmill played an active role in Dutch life have long since passed.

Barely one thousand windmills remain, but they are popular tourist attractions throughout the Dutch countryside and the towns. One of the major sights of the Rotterdam area, for instance, is the complex of large drainage mills along the Kinderdijk (KIN-der-dayk). Today many replicas and models of windmills are found in the gardens of suburban homes.

CREATING LAND

Land reclamation takes place in distinct stages. First, dikes are built around the area to be reclaimed. Then, water in the enclosed area is pumped out until dry land—the polder—starts to appear. To keep the polder dry, a network of small canals is constructed to drain the water into collector canals. From here the water is pumped to canals outside and above the polder, to be carried to sea. As rain, sea, or river water continually seeps into the polder, pumping is maintained daily.

Even after the polder's surface has dried, it is still unsuitable for agriculture due to the salt residue left by the sea. Coarse grass is planted and left to grow for a few years. This slowly eliminates the salt and helps to bind the soil together. Rain and continuous pumping further remove all traces of salt. Finally, the land is turned over to agriculture and settlement.

One of the largest reclamation projects occurred in 1932 after the damming of the Zuiderzee. Once this was turned into a large inland lake, four large polders were reclaimed and drained: the Wieringermeer, the North-East, South, and East Flevoland polders. These four polders have increased the country's land area by about 407,000 acres (165,000 hectares), nearly 5 percent of the country's total land area.

This photograph from 1932 shows farmers working to dam the Zuiderzee.

THE DELTA PROJECT

The Delta Project in Zeeland Province was devised to prevent any further disasters like the 1953 flood, which killed over 1,800 people in the Netherlands. The plan envisaged the construction of a series of dams where the Rhine and Scheldt rivers open into the sea, connecting the low islands facing the North Sea to create a barrier between the coastline and the sea.

Three artificial islands were constructed on existing sandbanks to shield the estuaries from the sea. However, many people objected to the enclosure of what they regarded as a unique and beautiful area, and there was also pressure to allow commercial fishing to continue. Eventually an open dam or storm-surge barrier was built across the Eastern Scheldt—2 miles (3.2 km) long with sixty-five concrete piers, between which sixty-two steel gates are suspended. These vertical gates can be lowered to keep out floodwater. Dams and secondary dikes were also built in other parts of Zeeland Province.

EARTHQUAKES IN THE GRONINGEN GAS FIELDS

The Netherlands is rich in a valuable resource: natural gas. According to the Dutch government, around 50 percent of the energy used in the country is supplied by natural gas extraction. This extraction has consequences, however, and these consequences alter the very geography of the Netherlands. Since 1991, large-scale extraction in the Groningen gas fields has led to earthquakes, sometimes even as many as one hundred earthquakes per year. The most severe earthquake had a magnitude of 3.5 on the Richter scale, which means people living near the gas fields faced damage to their homes.

In response to concerns about the property damage and the long-term effects of gas extraction in Groningen, the Dutch government pledged to reduce gas production in the region. In June 2015, the government decided to lower production by 10 billion cubic meters (353 billion cubic feet). The government's official statement reads, "Gas extraction in the province of Groningen is causing earthquakes that damage buildings and houses. To make the region safer and more liveable for residents, the government has decided to extract less gas. It has also appointed a national coordinator to oversee operations."

CLIMATE

The climate in the Netherlands is typical of coastal northern Europe—mild, wet, and cool. Although the Netherlands is part of the European mainland, the Gulf Stream and the westerly sea winds protect the country from the extremes of the central European winter.

Average rainfall is evenly spread over the year at 30 inches (76 cm). Temperatures rarely reach extremes of either heat or cold, although average temperatures in Europe have gradually risen over the past two hundred years. Amsterdam's average winter temperature in January is about 41 degrees Fahrenheit (5 degrees Celsius). Summer temperatures in July hover around 69°F (21°C).

There is little variation in climate from one region to another, although maritime effects are less noticeable farther inland. The mild, damp climate supports grasslands and livestock farming, and favors horticulture.

Mild winters mean that shipping is seldom icebound. On the other hand, frequent changes in weather—another result of being close to the North

Sea—often give rise to fog and slippery road conditions in winter. The flat areas of North and South Holland facing the North Sea are very windy, and as a result, wind turbines produce significant amounts of electricity and are frequently sited in this region.

WILDLIFE

The Netherlands is such a crowded country that wildlife has to fit in wherever it can. Wildlife mainly takes the form of birds, fish, and small, rather than large, animals.

Historically, cormorants have competed with fishermen and were viewed as pests.

Special areas have been created to protect flowers and trees, wildlife, and natural habitats. Hawks, cormorants, swans, ducks, and geese abound in these sanctuaries, as do small mammals such as squirrels. In addition, wading birds can be found in large numbers on the mud flats at the mouths of the many rivers. Foxes, boars, red deer, and the dormice are found in the higher provinces.

Land reclamation and the construction of dams have had an adverse effect on birds, marine creatures, and coastal flora. Most early dams were solid, except for a few with locks to serve coastal shipping. Although solid dams were effective in protecting the coastline, they had certain disadvantages, especially for species of birds that depended for their food on the continual covering and uncovering of mud banks formed by the tide. In addition, the dammed lakes slowly lost their salt content, posing a potential threat to the well-being of both the oyster population and the fishermen who depended on them for their living. As time passed, however, it became apparent that oysters were able to cope with the tideless conditions. Moreover, when the wading birds left, other birds, notably flamingos, moved in to take their place. Nature has adapted to the new conditions, but the Dutch authorities still receive complaints from environmentalists about the long- and short-term effects of the dams.

NOTABLE CITIES

The densest concentration of population in the Netherlands is found in the Randstad (ROHN-stadt, meaning Rim City) area. This stretches from Amsterdam to Rotterdam and includes the towns of Haarlem, Leiden, The Hague, and Utrecht (OOH-trekht).

AMSTERDAM Amsterdam, the capital of the Netherlands, straddles the IJ and Amstel rivers and is named after a dam on the Amstel River. This city of 1.1 million residents is surrounded by a network of canals and encircled by tall, elegant buildings. In the sixteenth century, Amsterdam became the center of economic prosperity in the Netherlands, and in the nineteenth century, it also became the diamond center of the world.

Schiphol (SHIP-hol) Airport, south of the city, is one of the most important airport hubs in Europe. The tourist industry has added to Amsterdam's importance. Events such as film festivals, flower parades, and outdoor concerts are some of the attractions for tourists as well as locals looking for entertainment.

THE HAGUE Although it is not the capital of the Netherlands, the government and administration of the country is in The Hague. The city's official name is 'S Gravenhage (SGRAH-ven-HAH-geh), but it is commonly called Den Haag (dun HAAGH) by the Dutch.

International organizations such as the International Court of Justice (part of the United Nations) and the International Institute of Social Studies are located in The Hague, which has a population of 650,000.

ROTTERDAM Rotterdam is the second-largest city in the Netherlands and home to one of the world's largest ports. It lies on the Nieuwe Maas River about 19 miles (30 km) from the North Sea, and has a population of 993,000. Rotterdam is connected to the industrial heartland of Europe by an extensive system of canals linked to the Rhine River.

UTRECHT The fourth-largest city in the Netherlands, Utrecht is an ancient city dating back to Roman times. The city's university was founded in 1636 and is the second oldest in the country. The Old Canal flows through the city center well below street level. Utrecht's industries produce a variety of manufactured goods. It has a population of 336,000.

MAASTRICHT Maastricht was initially a Roman town guarding an important crossing of the Maas River. Due to its proximity to Belgium and Germany, it is a cosmopolitan city with its own dialect, a diverse architectural style, and a rich international cuisine. Maastricht is largely Catholic, in contrast to the Protestant north. Today, the town is an important trading and industrial center specializing in ceramics, papermaking, and cement. It has a population of 122,000.

INTERNET LINKS

www.britannica.com/place/Netherlands
The Encyclopedia Britannica's entry about the Netherlands includes a summary about the country's geography, "Quick Facts," images, videos, and audio.

https://www.cia.gov/library/publications/the-world-factbook/geos/nl.html
The CIA's official website provides maps, photos, and details about the Netherlands' terrain.

travel.nationalgeographic.com/travel/countries/netherlands-guide
National Geographic's "Netherlands" features an in-depth guide about the impact of the country's geographical makeup on its development.

HISTORY

Charlemagne (circa 747-814) is just one of the Netherlands' many early conquerors.

2

T HE DUTCH HAVE A LONG AND storied history that involves key players in world events like Charlemagne, William of Orange, and the Dutch East India Company. The early days of the nation were a time of constant invasion, and the leadership of the Netherlands switched hands with each new invader. These times of invasion led to the unique culture of the Dutch.

In more modern times, famous Dutch citizens like Rembrandt and Anne Frank captured the country's transformation into an independent constitutional monarchy in the midst of a conflicted and changing world. Today, as a powerful and robust country, the Netherlands makes history with its navigation of complex issues within the European Union.

EARLY OCCUPATION

Lacking mountains and other such natural borders, the Netherlands has been invaded and occupied by foreign powers for much of its history. From the first to the fourth centuries, the Romans occupied the Low Countries and dominated the local populations, including Celtic tribes such as the Batavi and the Frisians. The Frisians are believed to have pioneered the building of dikes. Over two thousand years ago, they built mounds of earth along the marshy coast of Friesland to keep the

The history of the Netherlands has been connected with that of its neighbors, Belgium and Luxembourg, for the past two thousand years. For many centuries, these three countries were known collectively as the Low Countries.

Scandinavian Vikings are depicted here in a painting called *The Sea Warriors.*

sea out. Sometimes, by piercing the dikes and flooding the land, water was used to keep the enemy out.

From the fifth century onward, the Germanic Saxons and Franks occupied most of the country, except for the lands held by the Frisians. In the eighth century, Charlemagne, a Frankish king, incorporated the Low Countries into his Holy Roman Empire, and in the ninth century, Vikings from Scandinavia made the Utrecht area one of their bases.

Between the tenth and thirteenth centuries, present-day provinces were carved out and stabilized by a succession of princes, bishops, and counts. From the fourteenth to the sixteenth centuries, the Low Countries came under a succession of foreign rulers—the French Burgundians, the Austrian Hapsburgs, and the Spanish.

THE MIDDLE AGES

During the Middle Ages, the area now known as the Netherlands was split into several autonomous duchies and counties, in addition to land ruled by the bishop of Utrecht. The French Burgundians controlled northern France and what is now Belgium. Their power expanded to the present-day provinces of Limburg and North Brabant in the late fourteenth century. In the fifteenth century, this was extended to Holland, Zeeland, and Gelderland.

In 1477, Mary, daughter and heir of the duke of Burgundy, married into the Hapsburg family of Austria, and as a result, the Low Countries came under Hapsburg control. Mary's son, Philip, later married into the Spanish royal family, and Philip's son, Charles, ascended the Spanish throne. In 1515, Charles I of Spain inherited the Low Countries from his father. The Low Countries were nominally Catholic, although Amsterdam was tolerant of Protestants and became the focus of much Protestant inward migration.

DUTCH REVOLT

As Protestantism spread through the largely Catholic European countries, Charles I became concerned about a possible Protestant revolt. As such, strict Catholicism was imposed on Amsterdam. In 1555, he abdicated in favor of his son, Philip II. A devout Catholic, Philip condemned thousands of Dutch Protestants to death for heresy.

In 1567, he sent the Duke of Alva to strengthen Catholic control of Amsterdam. However, the Dutch did not take kindly to being given orders by Philip, a distant, foreign king who had been born and brought up in Spain. In 1568, Prince William of Orange raised an army to fight the Spanish, marking the beginning of the Eighty Years' War of independence. In addition to religious concerns, Philip wanted to limit the rapidly expanding Dutch economy that threatened Spanish interests.

Charles I of Spain ruled the Netherlands from 1515 to 1555.

By 1572, William had liberated Zeeland and Holland, and in 1573, he defeated the Duke of Alva's army in a battle at Zuiderzee. Although both the Dutch Catholics and Protestants joined forces to fight the Spanish, they remained divided about religion. The northern Dutch provinces were largely Protestant, while the south was mainly Catholic.

In 1581, seven northern provinces signed the Union of Utrecht treaty, under which they declared themselves the independent United Provinces of the Netherlands. The southern provinces—present-day Belgium and Luxembourg—remained under Spanish Catholic domination. However, Spain continued its land and sea attacks to regain control of the northern provinces. The Eighty Years' War came to an end in 1648, when Spain finally recognized the Netherlands' independence.

THE GOLDEN AGE

The United Provinces controlled shipping on the Rhine River due to their location. Amsterdam began to prosper as a port, and the stage was set for Dutch adventurers to explore Asia and the Americas and to open up new areas for trade.

In the seventeenth century, Dutch merchants established trading posts all over the world, from the Far East to the Caribbean. The Dutch East India

Company (Vereenigde Oost-Indische Compagnie, or the VOC) was founded in Amsterdam in 1602 to handle trade between the United Provinces and territories in the Indian Ocean. The Dutch West India Company was established in 1621 to trade with the Americas and Africa. As commerce expanded, the United Provinces became extremely wealthy.

The newfound prosperity and religious tolerance of the Dutch sparked a flourishing spiritual and cultural life. This golden age produced many great Dutch painters—particularly Rembrandt van Rijn, Jan Vermeer, Frans Hals, and Jacob van Ruisdael.

In addition, the Golden Age was notable for its contributions in furniture making, gold- and silversmithing, and architecture. Scientific advances were also made. Antonie van Leeuwenhoek invented the microscope and studied microbiology.

WAR AND THE END OF THE GOLDEN AGE

The Netherlands' prosperity led to conflicts with other European countries—wars with the British and French, continuing struggles with Spain, and opportunist forays by the Germans.

The Dutch and British went to war twice for control of the sea. In the First Anglo-Dutch War, the Dutch Admiral Maarten Tromp had to yield, but in 1667, Admiral Michiel de Ruyter made a daring raid into the River Medway, near London—the only time foreign guns were fired in the British capital.

The War of the Spanish Succession, where the Dutch, English, and French all laid claim to the throne of Spain, broke out at the turn of the eighteenth century and dragged on for twelve years. This war drained Dutch finances and led indirectly to the end of the Golden Age.

THE DUTCH DOMINION

Dutch interests overseas expanded rapidly during the seventeenth century as explorers braved the unknown to open trading routes and new settlements. As a result of an embargo on Dutch trade with Spain and Portugal, the Dutch turned their attention to direct trade with the East.

MARE LIBERUM

The Vereenigde Oost-indische Compagnie, or Dutch East India Company, shaped Dutch history from its founding in 1602 until its dissolution in 1799. Yet the Netherlands was not the only nation of the era eager to seek fortune through international trade. Naval battles were common at the time between vessels from different nations. These battles were so common, in fact, that a Dutch scholar named Hugo Grotius wrote a book called Mare Liberum *(Latin for "freedom of the seas"). Grotius was the first person to state that oceans should be open rather than owned by a particular country. Legal scholars say that Grotius's book marks the beginning of modern international law. Grotius clearly states his belief in the treatise:*

> My intention is to demonstrate briefly and clearly that the Dutch—that is to say, the subjects of the United Netherlands—have the right to sail to the East Indies, as they are now doing, and to engage in trade with the people there. I shall base my argument on the following most specific and unimpeachable axiom of the Law of Nations, called a primary rule or first principle, the spirit of which is self-evident and immutable, to wit: Every nation is free to travel to every other nation, and to trade with it.

While Mare Liberum *might be straightforward and accessible, it's not concise. The book, which was commissioned by the VOC to be a short legal document, is thirteen chapters long!*

In 1596, Cornelis de Houtman arrived in Java and established Dutch occupation in the Indonesian archipelago. Batavia (now Jakarta, capital of Indonesia) was established by Jan Pieterszoon Coen in 1619 and became the administrative center of the colony. Known as the Dutch East Indies, it remained a Dutch colony until 1949, when it became independent.

Dutch adventurers and traders explored the world in their sailing ships. In 1596, Willem Barents discovered Spitsbergen in the Arctic Ocean while searching for a northeast route to India. New Zealand was discovered by another Dutch sailor, Abel Tasman, who also gave his name to the island of Tasmania in Australia. The Cape Colony, now Cape Town in South Africa, was founded by Jan van Riebeeck in 1652 as a stopping point on the route to India.

The Dutch first settled on Manhattan Island in 1625, calling their settlement Nieuw Amsterdam. In 1626, Peter Minuit of the Dutch West India Company purchased Manhattan from the Native Americans for the equivalent of $24. Nieuw Amsterdam was taken by the British in 1664 and renamed New York after the Duke of York, later King James II. In exchange, the Dutch acquired Dutch Guiana (modern-day Suriname) in South America.

In South America, the Guinea coast was occupied by the Dutch in 1613. Ten years later, parts of Brazil also became a Dutch colony. In North America, Nieuw Amsterdam was founded in 1625, and twenty years later, Peter Stuyvesant became its last Dutch governor. By 1634, the Dutch also had a string of small possessions in the Antilles in the eastern Caribbean, many of which are still part of the Netherlands today, though they are now autonomous countries.

INDEPENDENCE

The Dutch remained independent for 150 years, until the rise of the French Empire in Napoleonic times. After a French army occupied the United Provinces in 1795, the conquered territory was renamed the Batavian Republic and became a vassal state of the French Empire. In 1806, Napoleon installed his brother Louis as king of Holland, and in 1810, the country was annexed to France.

The French occupation ended in 1814 when the Kingdom of the Netherlands declared independence. The new country united the present-day Netherlands, Belgium, and Luxembourg. Unlike the previous republican system, where a *stadhouder*, or governor, ruled the country, it became a constitutional monarchy. The Netherlands invited former stadhouder William IV, a descendant of Prince William of Orange, to return from exile and reign over their new constitutional monarchy as King William I. During the nineteenth century, the parliament became stronger as the sovereign's powers were slowly curbed. In 1814, a new constitution decreed that the monarch should govern and that ministers should be accountable to the sovereign. The constitution of 1848, which is still in force today, made ministers accountable to an elected parliament.

In 1839, the southern Catholic provinces of the Netherlands gained independence and became the country of Belgium. Luxembourg became independent in 1890, when Wilhelmina became queen of the Netherlands. Due to an ancient law that prevented women from ruling the grand duchy, Luxembourg could not recognize Wilhelmina as the monarch and ended its union with the Netherlands.

Louis Bonaparte was king of Holland for only four years.

WORLD WAR I AND WORLD WAR II

Located between Britain and Germany—opposing countries in World War I—the Netherlands was able to maintain its neutrality during the Great War. However, during World War II, the Netherlands was invaded by Germany in May 1940. After the bombing of Rotterdam, the Dutch capitulated in the face of Germany's overwhelming military power. Queen Wilhelmina and the Dutch government set up a government-in-exile in England, and her daughter, Princess Juliana, went to Canada with her family for safety.

German occupation of the Netherlands lasted five years and inflicted misery, humiliation, and degradation on the population. Food shortages, lack of freedom, forced labor, censorship, and curfews were common. The deportation of Dutch Jews to concentration camps deprived the country of a well-integrated and vigorous minority. A Dutch resistance movement soon sprang up, but the Germans retaliated with random killings after each act of defiance.

Anne Frank, who went into hiding in Amsterdam during World War II, is an important icon of the Holocaust.

Unfortunately for the Dutch, a bold plan by the Allies to bring the war to a swift end in September 1944 failed. The "Bridge Too Far" operation—a plan to capture the Arnhem bridge over the Rhine and isolate German troops—was a disaster. In the terrible winter that followed, thousands of Dutch people died of starvation. Many were reduced to eating tulip bulbs to survive.

By the end of the German occupation, Dutch cities were in shambles, the economy was in ruins, and the population was starving. In April 1945, the Allies liberated the Netherlands, and food and other supplies poured in to relieve the suffering. Queen Wilhelmina and her government-in-exile returned to pick up the pieces and start the long task of reconstruction.

COLONIALISM COMES TO A CLOSE

Until World War II, the Netherlands held colonies in Southeast Asia, the Caribbean, and South America, but these territories sought independence after 1945. After fierce fighting, in 1949, the Netherlands was forced to recognize the independence of its colonies in Southeast Asia, which later formed the Republic of Indonesia. By the 1954 Charter for the Kingdom, Suriname and the Netherlands Antilles (Aruba, Curaçao, Bonaire, St. Eustatius, Saba, and St. Maarten) in the eastern Caribbean became partners with the Netherlands, although the Netherlands remained responsible for defense and foreign policy. Suriname became independent in 1975. The Netherlands Antilles dissolved in 2010 when the final remaining islands, Curaçao and St. Maarten, received autonomous status. The other islands had negotiated autonomy prior to that date, starting with Aruba in 1986.

MODERN HISTORY

Dependence on international trade has led the Dutch to take a particular interest in international law. Many international treaties are signed here and

The legal statuses of the islands that formerly constituted the Netherlands Antilles can be confusing. The Dutch government describes the shift best:

> Aruba, Curaçao, St. Maarten, Bonaire, Saba, and St. Eustatius form the Dutch Caribbean within the Kingdom of the Netherlands. The Kingdom of the Netherlands is a comprehensive sovereign state made up of four countries of which the Netherlands is one. Aruba, Curaçao, and St. Maarten each form one of the three remaining constituent countries, while the other islands, Bonaire, St. Eustatius, and Saba, are Dutch overseas public bodies and as such are part of the country of the Netherlands. Collectively these three islands are known as the Caribbean Netherlands.

Together the Netherlands, Aruba, Curaçao, and St. Maarten are known as the Kingdom of the Netherlands. The islands that form the Caribbean Netherlands are considered part of the Netherlands itself. Sometimes the islands of the Caribbean Netherlands are called the "BES Islands," a name that comes from the first letter of each island's name. The former Netherlands Antilles is an important and often overlooked facet of the Kingdom of the Netherlands. The tropical parts of the kingdom point to the Netherlands' long history as a nation of explorers.

the International Court of Justice is located in The Hague. The Netherlands is also part of many international organizations. These include the European Union, the United Nations, the North Atlantic Treaty Organization (NATO), the Organization for Economic Cooperation and Development, and the Benelux Customs Union (together with Belgium and Luxembourg). Dutch support for disarmament, human rights, and the elimination of racial discrimination is widely respected.

After the Dutch referendum on the EU constitution, a UK newspaper called the Guardian *reported, "The Dutch revolt against their rulers in The Hague and Brussels is without parallel. For fifty years, the Netherlands has been a stronghold of European integration and the home to the Maastricht Treaty that produced the euro single currency—the most striking instrument of unification."*

During the 1990s, the Netherlands was a major force for the economic and political unification of Europe. However, recent political upheavals—such as the assassination of politician Pim Fortuyn in 2002, who was known for his controversial views on immigration and Islam—have somewhat tarnished the impression of Dutch commitment to freedom of opinion. In October 2005, suspects were detained in various Dutch cities for allegedly planning terror attacks, and in 2014, 196 Dutch nationals died aboard Malaysia Airlines Flight MH17. The flight is understood to have been accidentally shot down by Russia during their conflict with Ukraine. The tragedy caused rising tensions between the Netherlands and Russia.

THE EUROPEAN UNION

The Netherlands is a founding member of the European Union (EU), which began as the European Economic Community (EEC). The EEC was set up in 1958 to facilitate the free trade of goods and services among member countries. Initially there were six members—Belgium, West Germany, France, Italy, Luxembourg, and the Netherlands. By 2013, membership of the union increased to twenty-eight countries, with the most recent addition of Croatia.

In late 1991, when the Netherlands held the presidency of the then—EEC, it promoted the Maastricht Treaty, which called for the evolution of a supranational federal Europe, including full monetary union with a common currency and the removal of all trade barriers. The Maastricht Treaty created the European Union, which incorporated the European Coal and

Steel Community, the European Atomic Energy Commission, and the EEC. The European Union came into being on November 1, 1993 and is, in effect, an enlarged and more powerful EEC with a common foreign and security policy and an agreement to cooperate on justice and home affairs issues. Euro currency bills and coins were introduced into general circulation in 2002 and are accepted in several EU countries.

Dutch mourners mark the loss of those aboard Flight MH17.

In 2005, Dutch and French voters overwhelmingly voted against the proposed EU constitution, preventing the constitution's ratification. The Dutch opposition to the constitution came as a surprise from the nation that had pioneered the unity of Europe.

INTERNET LINKS

www.bbc.co.uk/history/people/william_iii_of_orange
This website offers a comprehensive look at the life and impact of William III from the BBC.

www.history.com/this-day-in-history/new-amsterdam-becomes-new-york
History.com explores how New Amsterdam became New York City after the Dutch lost control of the territory in 1664.

www.rijksmuseum.nl/en/explore-the-collection/timeline-dutch-history
The Rijksmuseum, the foremost museum in the Netherlands, condenses Dutch history into a comprehensive timeline.

faculty.webster.edu/woolflm/netherlands.html
Dr. Linda M. Woolf's "Survival and Resistance: The Netherlands Under Nazi Occupation" gives context for *The Diary of Anne Frank*.

GOVERNMENT

The complex of Dutch parliament buildings is called the Binnenhof.

3

THE DUTCH GOVERNMENT IS A blend of monarchy and democracy not found elsewhere in the world. The Dutch support the king as a leader who swears to protect the constitution of the Netherlands. It's a system that has worked for hundreds of years, and only the most extreme politicians have called for the end of the monarchy—a minority view that is unlikely to take hold. The government is more than the king, though. Ministers (including the prime minister), parliament, and advisory/investigative bodies work together to make new laws and re-evaluate established ones.

PARLIAMENT

The Dutch parliament is called the States General, a term left over from feudal times, when representatives of various estates were summoned by their lords to discuss political and financial matters. The States General has two chambers—a Lower and an Upper House.

The Lower House has 150 members who are directly elected by the population for a four-year term. Universal male suffrage was introduced in 1917. Women were given the vote two years later, and until 1970 voting in a general election was compulsory by law.

The Upper House has seventy-five members elected by provincial councils for a four-year term. These councils are also elected by universal suffrage, so both houses have virtually the same political composition. The States General, the king, and the ministers form the legislature.

Legislation is introduced by the executive branch to the Lower House, which can amend a bill or refuse to pass it. The Lower House may also introduce legislation, although this right is seldom exercised. Legislation passed by the Lower House goes to the Upper House, which can vote on bills but may not amend them. When a bill has passed through both houses, it goes to the monarch for assent. It becomes law only when both the monarch and the responsible minister sign it.

King Willem-Alexander (*left*) and Queen Beatrix (*center*) are just two generations of the Dutch monarchy.

THE EXECUTIVE BRANCH

After an election, the monarch appoints ministers on the recommendation of a *formateur* (form-a-TERH). According the government of the Netherlands, the formateur is "in most cases the intended Prime Minister." The parties forming the new government divide the cabinet posts between them based on the number of seats they have in parliament. Ministers are not members of parliament; they have the right to speak in the States General but not to vote.

The prime minister and other ministers form the cabinet and coordinate government policy. From 1994 to 2002, Wim Kok of the Labor Party was the prime minister. After the general election of 2002, a new coalition government was formed from an alliance of three political parties. The current prime minister is Mark Rutte of the People's Party for Freedom and Democracy.

King Willem-Alexander's home, Villa Eikenhorst.

THE INAUGURATION OF WILLEM-ALEXANDER

King Willem-Alexander was inaugurated on April 30, 2013, the day his mother officially abdicated. The ceremony was held in front of two thousand people, including government officials, the royal family, and even royalty from other countries. In his speech that historic day, King Willem-Alexander addressed his mother and commemorated her service to the country:

My dear Mother, as Queen you were fully conscious of the responsibilities attached to your position. You were utterly dedicated to the duties of your office. But you were also a daughter, a wife, a mother, and head of the family. And you have always sought to do full justice to each of those responsibilities … With the help of my father, you developed your own style as Queen. You never chose the easy path of fleeting popularity. You navigated stormy waters, charting a sure and steady course in the knowledge that you were part of a long tradition.

Now, I follow in your footsteps. And I have a clear picture of my duties. No one knows what the future may hold. But wherever my path leads, and however long it may be, I will always carry with me your warmth and your wisdom.

I know that I speak for many in the Netherlands and in the Caribbean parts of our Kingdom when I say: thank you for all the wonderful years in which you served as our Queen.

Unlike in other monarchies, King Willem-Alexander was inaugurated, not crowned. These other monarchies use the term "coronation" to describe the ceremony during which a new ruler is crowned. In the Netherlands, however, when a new king or queen ascends to the throne, he or she is presented with a crown that is never worn. The process of inauguration is overseen by the Dutch parliament and involves a swearing-in process that is quite similar to the inauguration of a US president.

THE MONARCHY

The Dutch monarchy belongs to the House of Orange Nassau, which dates back to the sixteenth century. Its founder was Prince William of Orange.

In 1890 there was no male heir so the throne passed to the monarch's eldest daughter, Wilhelmina. Since then, the Netherlands has had two additional queens—Juliana became queen when Wilhelmina abdicated in 1948, and Beatrix succeeded to the throne when Juliana abdicated in 1980. Queen Beatrix's eldest son, Willem-Alexander, became king when she abdicated in 2013. In a political scene dominated by shifting alliances created by the system of proportional representation, the sovereign is the one fixed factor. The monarchy can, however, be abolished by an act of parliament. The Dutch would probably declare a republic if the House of Orange died out.

THE NEW KING

In addition to being the Netherlands' first king in 123 years, Willem-Alexander became the youngest monarch in Europe when he was crowned. King Willem-Alexander vowed to be a progressive ruler, telling his subjects that the use of "your majesty" to address him was now optional.

Although King Willem-Alexander is one of the wealthiest men in Europe, lavish display of wealth is definitely not the style of the Dutch monarchy. The family is admired because its members live much like ordinary citizens. The Royal Palace in Amsterdam, for example, is used only for official functions. The king's home is not a palace but a house called Villa Eikenhorst.

Affection for the monarchy, however, does not mean that it is above criticism. In the 1970s, when Prince Bernhard, Queen Juliana's husband, was implicated in a business scandal, he had to withdraw from public life.

ADVISORY AND INVESTIGATIVE BODIES

Three other government institutions—the Council of State, the Court of Audit, and the national ombudsman—play an important part in Dutch public life.

The Council of State consists of the king as president of the council, a vice president responsible for the daily operations of the council, and up to ten members. Members are chosen for their experience in administrative matters. The council is the highest advisory body in the state and must be consulted before any legislation goes to the States General.

The Court of Audit has three members. It monitors the management of state funds. The court submits an annual report to the king and the Lower House, and this is made available to the public. Members are appointed for life, and they retire when they reach the age of seventy.

In 1982, the Dutch government created the post of national ombudsman. The word "ombudsman" (ohm-BOODS-mahn) is of Swedish origin and means an investigator of public complaints. Accordingly, the Dutch ombudsman is an independent officer who investigates complaints made by members of the public against the executive branch. The ombudsman has wide-ranging powers to examine any aspect of the relationship of the government to the ordinary citizen.

Reinier van Zutphen is the current National Ombudsman.

BALANCING POWER

As with all modern democracies, the government of the Netherlands has a system of checks and balances to ensure that political power is exercised according to the law. The government is responsible to the people through their elected representatives in the States General.

The States General has three ways of checking the power of the government: First, it has the right to set a budget. Second, it can set up independent inquiries on government matters. Finally, it has the right to question ministers and state secretaries about present or future policies.

PROVINCIAL GOVERNMENT

The country is divided into twelve provinces, each administered by a provincial council directly elected by residents of the province. Elections are held every four years under the system of proportional representation. The most densely populated provinces have more council members under this proportional representation system.

Council members elect a provincial executive from among themselves to handle day-to-day administration in the province. The chair of both the council and the executive board is called the king's commissioner and is appointed by the Crown. The council chooses which of its members will represent the province in the Upper House of the States General.

MUNICIPAL AUTHORITIES

Each town and village in the country has a municipal council. Council members are elected by proportional representation every four years. The largest municipal council has forty-five members, and the smallest has only seven. Daily administration is the responsibility of the burgomaster (or mayor) and the aldermen. The burgomaster is appointed for six years by the king on the recommendation of the government, and aldermen are elected from among the members of the municipal council.

In recent years, municipalities have found it increasingly beneficial to join forces in tackling common problems related to zoning, transportation, and the environment.

WATER CONTROL BOARDS

Water control boards, or *waterschappen* (WAH-ter-sghap-pen), are among the oldest democratic institutions in the Netherlands. They are responsible for managing water in the polders, and their tasks also include the construction and maintenance of roads, bridges, and other public works. Their prime role is the prevention of flooding.

Members of water boards are elected by property owners of the area in question. The most important boards are those near the sea, the major rivers, and the IJsselmeer.

Flooding can cause catastrophic damage to homes and buildings located near the water.

THE COURT SYSTEM

The Dutch legal system is relatively straightforward, and great emphasis is put on speed, simplicity, and the independence of judicial officials. Besides the subdistrict courts, district courts, courts of appeal, and the Supreme Court, specialized administrative tribunals also deal with social insurance, civil service, and other social and welfare matters. Judges make all court decisions. The Supreme Court is responsible for deciding if the law has been properly applied.

Binnenhof palace (pictured here) and the Dutch Supreme Court are located in The Hague.

INTERNET LINKS

www.economist.com/topics/dutch-politics
The *Economist*'s site features a roundup of articles about politics in the Netherlands.

www.government.nl
The Netherlands' official government website (in English).

www.houseofrepresentatives.nl/how-parliament-works/democracy-netherlands
"How Parliament Works" breaks down Dutch democracy.

www.the-netherlands.org
The page of the embassy of the Kingdom of the Netherlands includes up-to-date information about industry, culture, travel, and breaking news.

ECONOMY

The Port of Rotterdam is Europe's largest port.

4

THE ECONOMY OF THE NETHERLANDS is varied, encompassing everything from fishing to technological innovation. Yet the diversity of the Dutch economy has not been able to protect it from the fluctuation of world markets. Since 2008 the Dutch economy has been plagued by hardship, including three recessions, the last of which began to ease in 2014. Now the Greek debt crisis has affected all of Europe and led Prime Minister Mark Rutte to make decisions that have both economic and political consequences.

In spite of an uncertain economic future, the Dutch continue to innovate, manufacture goods, take advantage of natural resources, and act as a major trading hub for Europe and the world.

IMPORTS AND EXPORTS

With a handful of seaports, five international airports, 6,500 inland vessels, thousands of road transportation companies, and an extensive railway system, the Netherlands has often been called the "Gateway to Europe."

The majority of the Netherlands' trade is with EU countries, mainly Germany, Belgium, France, Italy, and the United Kingdom.

The Netherlands' location has made it one of Europe's great trading nations. Entrepôt trade—trade based on the transit of goods between Europe and the rest of the world—accounts for much of the country's national income. Most of this trade goes through Rotterdam's Europoort, one of the busiest ports in the world.

The Dutch pride themselves on the high-tech inventions of their countrymen. Groundbreaking technology like Wi-Fi and DVDs are just two examples of Dutch innovations. Bluetooth was invented by Jaap Haartsen in 1994. Haartsen's achievement led him all the way to induction in the US National Inventors Hall of Fame in 2015.

One reason for the impressive number of patents held by Dutchmen is that companies like tech giant Philips are headquartered in the Netherlands. In fact, Eindhoven is home to Brainport, the Netherlands' answer to Silicon Valley.

The Netherlands is the second biggest exporter of fruits and vegetables. Other exports include machinery and transportation equipment, food and chemicals, energy, and metals. Major imports are machinery and electrical equipment, food, beverages, tobacco, manufactured goods, transportation equipment, and energy.

The bulk of the Netherlands' trade goes through Rotterdam. Lying at the mouth of the Rhine's tributary, Rotterdam's Europoort is one of the largest port complexes in the world, extending for 21 miles (34 km) from the city to the Hook of Holland.

TRANSPORTATION

The Netherlands has had an extensive canal system to transport goods and passengers for hundreds of years. The canal system, much widened and modernized, still handles a large volume of heavy goods—cargo can be transported along canals and rivers within the country and as far inland as Germany and Switzerland. Dutch carriers account for about half the international transport by water within the EU. Most cargo goes by way of the Rhine River.

On the roads, Dutch haulers handle about one-third of international road freight within the EU. In the air, the Royal Dutch Airlines (or KLM) is one of the best-known airlines in the world. The Netherlands' aircraft manufacturer—Fokker—produces mainly civil transport and small regional aircraft. It was taken over in 1996 by another Dutch company, Stork Aerospace, to form Stork Fokker.

TECHNOLOGY AND MANUFACTURING

Most industries are concentrated in urban centers, such as Amsterdam, Utrecht, Haarlem, Rotterdam, and The Hague. Manufactured products include textiles, synthetic fibers, chemicals, and metal products. Other important industries include transportation, agri-industrial products, petroleum products, and rubber. Since the Netherlands is an important shipping nation, shipbuilding is a key industry.

In electronics, Philips of Eindhoven is a multinational company that is world famous for manufacturing electrical and electronic products. Unilever is another well-known Dutch company producing foods and detergents. Royal Dutch Shell is one of the world's largest oil- and gas-producing companies and is also based in the Netherlands.

ENERGY

The Netherlands has extensive oil and gas fields—nearly 22,000 square miles (57,000 sq km) in the North Sea—and is a leading producer of natural gas. Natural gas production in 2014 was nearly 2.5 trillion cubic feet (70.3 billion cubic meters) from mainland and offshore fields.

Although natural gas is used to produce electricity in 95 percent of all homes, over half of gas production is exported. However, the Netherlands' oil reserves are much smaller. Dutch oil wells supply 20 percent of domestic requirements, and the remainder has to be imported.

Since 1973 the government has followed a policy designed to reduce dependence on imported supplies. Intensive energy-saving campaigns have been conducted, and steps have been taken to develop alternative sources of power based on environment-friendly sources such as the wind. The Dutch had two nuclear power plants, but one was shut down in 1997. The other continues to produce energy for the country today.

In 1973, the global oil crisis led to an increasing interest in developing alternative sources of power. This event, along with environmental concerns, has stimulated the Dutch to develop wind turbines for generating electricity. Electricity generated by wind is not cheap, and there are concerns over noise

As of 2014, wind turbines provide 5.2 percent of the Netherlands' electricity.

pollution as well as hazards to birds caused by wind turbines. Nonetheless, the technology holds great potential.

Tall and slim, standing up to 650 feet (198 m) high with rotors nearly 500 feet (152 m) in diameter, wind turbines rise high above the polders of North Holland. Most have two or three propeller-like blades.

AGRICULTURE

About half the Netherlands' available land is used for agriculture—approximately 9,000 square miles (23,300 sq km) of land is dedicated to farming. Today, arable farming has become less important, though. The cultivation of crops such as rye and oats has declined, whereas that of corn for fodder has increased. Production of wheat, sugar beets, and potatoes has increased with larger areas under cultivation and greater yields per acre.

Dairy farming takes place mainly in the Friesland and North Holland provinces. In spite of a reduction in the number of dairy cows due to EEC quotas, improved efficiency has increased production of dairy products. With a large livestock industry—the Netherlands has had an enormous manure problem. Almost 100 million tons (90.7 million metric tons) of manure have to be disposed of every year. Half is used for fertilizer, while in the past, the remaining 50 million tons (45 million t) were left to seep into the ground, reducing land fertility and poisoning groundwater as a consequence. The Dutch government seeks to solve unfortunate problems through legislation and increased support for farmers.

The proportion of people working in agriculture has fallen to just 1.8 percent of the workforce. Most farms are small—averaging about 25 acres (10 ha)—but they are highly mechanized and efficient in labor and land use.

Most agricultural output is exported, adding €52.5 billion to the country's GDP. Although the Netherlands produces only 1 percent of the world's dairy

The Netherlands' unit of currency is the euro (€), which is accepted in eighteen other EU countries—Austria, Belgium, Cyprus, Estonia, Finland, France, Germany, Greece, Ireland, Italy, Latvia, Lithuania, Luxembourg, Malta, Portugal, Slovakia, Slovenia, and Spain. It was introduced into general circulation in 2002, and the old currency of the Netherlands, the guilder, has been phased out.

The euro is divided into 100 cents. Coins are issued in denominations of 1, 2, 5, 10, 20, and 50 cents; and 1 and 2 euros. Every euro coin from all countries adopting the single currency has one side in common showing the value of the coin, and one side unique to the country in which it was minted. Dutch euro coins feature a portrait of King Willem-Alexander.

Bank notes are issued in denominations of 5, 10, 20, 50, 100, 200, and 500 euros. These do not have an obvious indication of the country of issue, although this information is encoded in the serial numbers of the notes. Notes issued in the Netherlands have serial numbers beginning with the letter "P," while those from other EU countries begin with a different letter or number.

The national central banks of the nineteen countries using the euro, together with the European Central Bank (ECB), all play a decisive role in managing the euro. The ECB and the participating national banks are known collectively as the Eurosystem. Aside from ensuring a smooth transition in the adoption of the currency, the Eurosystem also looks into monetary policies and foreign exchange and payment systems. The Dutch national bank is called De Nederlandsche Bank.

output, it is the world's largest exporter of dairy products. While the number of cattle farms in the country has declined by half in the last twenty years, Dutch dairy products—made with imports from other countries—continue to rise.

THE GLASS CITY

Usually cultivated under glass in the Westland area between the Hook of Holland, The Hague, and Rotterdam, most of the Netherlands' flowers are exported to the EU.

TULIPS

Tulips are thought to have originated in Asia. They were brought to Europe from Turkey in the mid-sixteenth century and were cultivated in the western parts of the Netherlands.

In the 1630s, the rising demand for bulbs and the difficulties of obtaining flowers of consistent color and shape prompted a wave of wild speculation. This "tulip mania" saw prices rise dramatically, and family fortunes were both made and destroyed in the frantic trading that took place. At one point, a single white Semper Augustus bulb was sold for the equivalent of $5,000. After the economic climate settled, prices returned to sensible levels.

In this "Glass City," as the Westland area is called, greenhouses extend for over 23,000 acres (9,300 ha). Flowers are grown in gravel that is frequently flooded with water highly enriched with organic nutrients. Computers automatically regulate temperature and light by opening and closing vents and shutters in the roof and by switching on lights at night if necessary. They also control the water and nutrient supplies. Plants can be grown here year-round.

Outdoor horticultural production concentrates on cultivating a variety of bulbs—tulips, daffodils, hyacinths, crocuses, and other species. The flowers and plants are sold daily at large flower auctions. One of the most famous flower auctions takes place at Aalsmeer. More than twenty million cut flowers are sold here every day.

Growers load their flowers onto trolleys, which are linked together on an automatic rail system. As each trolley enters into the auction room, a large clock on the wall is set in motion. The hand begins at a figure indicating a starting price, which is lowered as the clock hand moves round. Buyers sit at their desks with fingers poised ready to press a button that will stop the clock at a price they are prepared to pay. This requires experience and quick reactions—pressing the button too early could commit buyers to too high a price, whereas pressing it too late would mean losing the flowers.

FISHING

Considering the length of the Netherlands' coastline, fishing plays a small part in the country's economy. This is due largely to over-fishing in the North Sea, land reclamation, and flood-prevention schemes that have cut off once-busy ports from the open sea. Even the freshwater fishing industry has declined, and famous fishing towns, such as Volendam and Marken, have come to rely on tourism rather than fishing.

INTERNET LINKS

www.hollandtrade.com
Hollandtrade.com is an official website created by the Dutch government to showcase "Dutch smart solutions to global challenges related to water, food, energy, mobility, health and a liveable habitat."

krugman.blogs.nytimes.com/2013/08/13/a-tale-of-two-flat-countries/?_r=0
In this blog post from the *New York Times*, economist Paul Krugman evaluates the effectiveness of the Netherlands' "financial austerity."

www.worldbank.org/en/country/netherlands
Raw economic data and summaries can be found on the World Bank's website.

www.wsj.com/articles/SB100014240527023048150045794185802 31847454
The *Wall Street Journal* reports on the Dutch economy's recovery from a recession.

According to the Ministry of Foreign Affairs, "The Netherlands is the world's second largest exporter of agricultural products, after the USA. Together with the USA and France, the Netherlands is one of the world's three leading producers of vegetables and fruit."

ENVIRONMENT

The Netherlands' diverse landscapes provide ideal homes for equally diverse plants and animals.

5

LIKE OTHER INDUSTRIALIZED NATIONS, the Netherlands is working toward finding a balance between economic prosperity and the preservation of its natural beauty. Agricultural by-products and drilling for natural gas are just two of the ways the environment is threatened in the Netherlands. The country has a lot to protect: it is home to over 24,500 species of animals. The unique geography of the Netherlands also fosters the growth of trees, flowers, and other plants. The country is famous for its tulips, though 10,000 other species of plants also grow there.

ECOSYSTEMS

As in other developed nations, the road to modernization in the Netherlands has been marked by a widespread destruction of forests and other natural habitats. At the beginning of the twentieth century, 28 percent of the Netherlands' land area was forested. By the mid-1970s the figure was down to 15 percent, and in 2011 only 10.82 percent of

European and other international regulations have set standards on the use of environmentally harmful substances. The Netherlands follows the Kyoto Protocol, the European Bird Directive, the European Habitat Directive, and several other cross-border environmental agreements.

the Netherlands was forested. Today the Netherlands' goal is to regrow its forests by 0.3 percent each year.

With scarce cultivable land area, farmers tried for decades to increase productivity by using excessive fertilizers and pesticides. While increasing agricultural output, this led to a tragic loss of habitats for native animal and plant species. Alarmed by this, the Dutch government devised a policy called Natuurbeleidsplan (Nature Policy Plan) in the 1990s. It established a national ecological network of nature preserves connected by lands acquired by the government and developed into natural habitats.

FAUNA

In the Netherlands, wildlife exists mainly in the form of fish, birds, small land mammals, and larger mammals such as deer, wild boar, and foxes. Because of the abundance of swamps and wetlands, the Netherlands has traditionally been a haven for birds.

The osprey, a migratory bird of prey, is one species that is observed more frequently today than it had been in the recent past. Ospreys are attracted to the Oostvaardersplassen, an expansive marsh in the center of the country. It has shallow water with plentiful fish, and the public is not allowed to enter most of the area, so the birds may feed undisturbed.

The Waddenzee Bird Sanctuary has been developed on the island of Terschelling. Natural areas have also been established for frogs, toads, snakes, hamsters, beavers, and other small land creatures. In March and April, toads migrate to mating grounds. Usually shy creatures, toads come out in large numbers during this time. Temporary road signs are erected to alert motorists of their presence.

REDUCING EMISSIONS

The Netherlands, like several other developed countries, is under pressure to reduce its use of fossil fuels to generate energy. As a signatory to the Kyoto Protocol—a 1997 agreement among 131 nations to reduce their emissions of greenhouse gases, which have been blamed for global warming and climate change—the Netherlands is required to cut back on its emissions of carbon dioxide. However, Dutch chemical, oil, and transportation industries consume so much energy that the emissions of carbon dioxide have stayed more or less the same since the Kyoto agreement.

Tourists can enjoy a guided walk through the bird sanctuary on Terschelling Island.

To reduce emissions without damaging industries, EU countries implemented a system for trading carbon dioxide emissions rights in 2005. Called the European Union Emissions Trading Scheme, it allows companies to buy and sell permits for emitting carbon dioxide. Companies are allotted permits to release a certain amount of this gas. They may either use them or sell them to other companies. This allows companies that have climate-friendly projects to sell their emissions rights to those that have a problem with emissions, allowing market forces to determine the price of cleaning the air. The European Climate Exchange is based in Amsterdam. Methane emissions are expected to come under the same rules as carbon dioxide emissions in the near future.

RENEWABLE ENERGY

The Energy Research Center of the Netherlands conducts research on the environment and energy, including wind energy, solar energy, renewable energy, and the clean burning of fossil fuels. The institute has connections

THE URGENDA RULING

In June 2015, The Hague District Court heard a case brought against the Dutch government by an activist group called Urgenda (whose name is inspired by the words "urgent" and "agenda"). Urgenda's complaint said that the Dutch government was not doing enough to protect citizens from the damage of greenhouse gases. The group felt that reducing emissions by 17 percent from the levels recorded in 1990—as proposed by the government—was not effective enough. Urgenda argued that the threat of climate change is a human rights issue.

When the court returned their ruling, the world was stunned. The Hague District Court ruled in favor of Urgenda and ordered the Dutch government to pay the group's legal expenses.

As a result of the ruling, the court decided the Dutch government must reduce emissions by 25 percent. Legal scholars believe that the Urgenda case will set precedents, not just in the Netherlands but around the world.

to universities and other facilities in various countries, and visiting scientists from overseas collaborate on efforts to develop Earth-friendly energy sources and reduce emissions of greenhouse gases. Industries that have energy-intensive production processes can also seek advice from the institute about achieving higher energy efficiency in their operations. The institute also advises the Dutch government on environmental policies.

The Netherlands has been associated with windmills for centuries and, in fact, windmills played an important role in the creation of polders by helping to drain out the water from them. However, windmills are not a reliable energy source for modern power needs because they work only when the wind blows; when the wind does not blow, alternative sources of energy are needed.

Windmills have now been replaced by wind farms with gigantic wind turbines, but even those have a long way to go before they start generating enough consistent power to significantly supplement other modern sources of energy. In 1995, the Dutch government announced that it intended to meet 10 percent of the country's energy needs with renewable energy by the year 2020. Officials said wind energy would play an important role in this development. Although growth in this area has been below expectations, there is hope that in a few years the wind will play a more significant role in sustainable power generation.

Two nuclear power plants—the Dodewaard and the Borssele—were built in the 1960s and 1970s to generate electricity for the Netherlands. Construction began on the Dodewaard plant in 1965. The plant was completed three years later and began generating electricity in October of 1968. The plant was active for twenty-nine years, though public opinion shifted against nuclear power after the Chernobyl disaster in Ukraine in 1986. The Dodewaard plant ultimately went offline due to protests and because the plant was losing money. Dodewaard needed extensive (and expensive) modernization to keep it running safely.

The Borssele Nuclear Power Plant generated 2.9 billion kWh of electricity in 2013.

The Borssele plant nearly faced a similar fate. The initial plan, formed in 1994, was that the power plant would be decommissioned by 2003. However, legal challenges to the decision to phase out the plant pushed the closure date back to 2013. Then, in 2006, an official inquiry found that the power plant was a positive force in the Dutch economy. The latest decision says the plant will stay on line until 2034. Today, the Borssele reactor generates nearly 4 percent of the electricity used in the Netherlands.

GOING GREEN

Residents of the Netherlands are, in general, aware of environmental issues and are diligent about recycling. They separate their garbage more precisely than do residents of the United States. Neighborhoods have communal bins where households and businesses deposit various categories of waste: paper, glass, and old clothing. Consumers are reimbursed for any plastic

The Dutch commute to work is unlike any other.

containers they return to the supermarket, such as beverage bottles and containers for food and other products.

Every couple of weeks, residents and businesses put out a bin containing chemical waste, ranging from batteries to cosmetics. And every week, households put out two containers of garbage, one containing "green" waste— food scraps, garden clippings, and other organic matter—and the second containing residual garbage that does not fit into any of the above categories.

In the inner city areas of Amsterdam, Rotterdam, The Hague, and Utrecht, many people prefer to ride bicycles rather than drive cars, to avoid the problems of traffic and parking. In less congested areas, too, some Dutch residents cycle to work or school—both for the exercise and in an attempt to be environmentally friendly. More than 80 percent of the population in the Netherlands owns at least one bicycle. An increasing number of residents are driving to work, but in 2013 there were still 26 percent of residents cycling to work.

ENVIRONMENTAL ISSUES IN THE CARIBBEAN NETHERLANDS

The countries formerly known as the Netherlands Antilles consist of the islands of St. Maarten, Saba, St. Eustatius, Curaçao, and Bonaire in the Caribbean Sea. While autonomous, these nations are still officially part of the Netherlands. Oil, offshore finance, and tourism are the main industries here. Visitors come from all over the world to experience the natural beauty of the islands and surrounding waters, renowned for their corals and abundance of marine life.

The islands have not had effective policies for garbage recycling and reduction, and as a result, there is a large volume of undisposed waste. Inadequately regulated oil production and transportation add their share of waste products. With tourism playing a major role in the islands' economy, the governments of the islands are understandably concerned.

The government formulated the Nature and Environment Policy Plan 2013—2017 to deal with waste, conserve natural resources, increase public awareness of environmental issues, and develop sustainable tourism in the Caribbean Netherlands.

Government initiatives aim to keep the beaches in the former Netherlands Antilles pristine.

INTERNET LINKS

www.ecn.nl/home
The Environmental Research Center of the Netherlands site allows browsing about the company, its policies, and its plans for the future.

www.government.nl/topics/environment
The Environment page on the Netherlands' official website examines the country's environmental policies.

www.pbl.nl/en
The PBL Netherlands Environmental Assessment Agency presents news related to the environment in English.

THE DUTCH

Over 40 percent of the Dutch population is twenty-five to fifty-four years old.

6

WHILE IT'S IMPOSSIBLE TO ASSIGN a quintessential Dutch identity to a population of almost 17 million people, there are characteristics that many Dutch people share. These characteristics include liberal social ideas. Dutch people pride themselves on living a balanced life and maintaining their humility. Many travelers also remark on the straightforwardness of the Dutch, which can sometimes be perceived as rudeness.

As more people immigrate to the Netherlands, the country is growing and changing. The idea of what it means to be Dutch is, too.

POPULATION CHANGES

The population has grown sevenfold since the first census was taken more than 150 years ago. In 1830, the Dutch numbered only 2.6 million, but improved medical care during the second half of the nineteenth century led to falling mortality rates and a rise in population. This growth meant that rural areas were less able to support the increasing number of people.

Up to the early twentieth century, migration to towns became common. Most people moved to urban areas in North and South Holland, but after World War II, thousands of Dutch also emigrated to Canada, the

Today the Netherlands has a population of over 16.9 million, which makes it one of the most densely populated countries in the world, with 1,295 people per square mile. In comparison, Japan has 904 people per square mile, France has 314, and the United States has only 91.

Drenthe, the least densely populated province, is in the northeast.

United States, South Africa, Australia, and New Zealand. Later in the 1950s, as the political situation in Europe stabilized, the number of emigrants decreased. In the 1960s and 1970s, there was an influx of immigrant workers from Mediterranean countries and former Dutch colonies such as Suriname. The late 1990s saw an influx of political refugees from Iraq and Afghanistan. In 2015, nearly forty thousand immigrants entered the Netherlands largely due to the Syrian refugee crisis. It remains to be seen how the country will handle such a large number of refugees.

Overall, the Netherlands is experiencing a falling birth rate and an aging population. In 1900, 44 percent of the population were below the age of twenty, and 6 percent were over sixty-four. By the end of the twentieth century, the figures were 24 percent and 14 percent, respectively.

DUTCH HERITAGE

The Dutch people are basically a Germanic people, descended from Frisians, Saxons, and Franks. They have been open to external influences for so long that many Dutch are of mixed European ancestry—French Huguenots, Salzburgers, Swiss, Germans, and Portuguese and Eastern European Jews.

During the twentieth century, the Netherlands' ethnic composition was changed by immigrants from its former colonies—Surinamese from South America and Indonesians from the former Dutch East Indies. Other immigrants have come from Turkey, Morocco, Germany, Britain, and other European countries. In the last few years there have been increasing numbers of immigrants from Afghanistan and Iraq. Today about 10 percent of the Dutch population is of non-Western descent. In 1970 there were fewer than 30 countries represented in the population, but today there are 110.

The greatest population concentration is in the three provinces of North Holland, South Holland, and Utrecht—nearly half of the population lives here.

The least densely populated province is Drenthe, which has only one-seventh the population density of South Holland.

THE DUTCH CHARACTER

Perhaps the most notable characteristics of the Dutch are their love of moderation and their respect for law and order. These values are accepted across the whole of society, from the highest to the lowest economic levels. The small size of their country has forced the Dutch to be realistic about liberty and individualism. Having created a country in which so many wish to live, they are highly organized in the way they run their private and national lives. These factors and their trading links with neighboring countries have made them practical people.

Queen Beatrix at her silver jubilee.

Although the native Dutch are quite homogeneous, people from different regions vary in character. In the south, people tend to be more easy-going and relaxed, while in the north, residents are influenced by the more formal reserve of their German neighbors.

At her silver jubilee in 2005, Queen Beatrix made an observation that "some of our matter-of-factness, austerity, and moderation—which were part of the Dutch character—have become less visible." She also urged her people to practice tolerance toward one another.

TRADITIONAL DRESS

Traditional costume is still worn in several towns and villages in the Netherlands. Although some people wear this on a regular basis, others only do so on special days and holidays. In the past, the number and variety of regional costumes were much higher than today, but those that remain illustrate the originality that makes Dutch local costume so attractive.

Women's costumes usually consist of a skirt, an apron, and a front-fastening jacket, often with short sleeves. Headdresses, on the other hand,

A SIGN OF WELLNESS?

The Dutch are known to be the tallest people in the world. The national average height for men is 6 feet 0.6 inches (185 cm) and 5 feet 9 inches (175 cm) for women. In comparison, the average height in the United States is 5 feet 9 inches (176.7 cm) for men and 5 feet 5 inches (163 cm) for women.

Auxologists are people who study human growth. They approach the examination of growth from biological, social, historical, and economic standpoints. Most believe that height is a measure of health and wellness. The height of the Dutch population has been attributed to the high standard of medical care, sensible diet, and healthy lifestyle and environment.

vary widely, including the winged caps of the Volendam women, the silver helmets worn at Staphorst, and the fitted lace caps covering the ears, which are typical of Zeeland Province.

Men's traditional dress usually consists of a black jacket and trousers, enlivened by a brightly colored shirt, rows of silver buttons on the jacket, and

A Dutch couple wears traditional clothing at a tulip festival.

THE HISTORY OF WOODEN SHOES

Klompen are sometimes referred to in English simply as "wooden shoes." Wooden clogs might not sound very comfortable to wear, but fans of the footwear cite the shoes' health benefits. Many say that clogs are superior to other shoes because the wood absorbs sweat. Klompen are worn less and less today, but according to archaeological evidence, the tradition of farmers wearing wooden clogs can be traced to at least 1230 CE. Mass-produced wooden shoes can be found primarily in souvenir shops around the Netherlands, though artisans still make klompen by hand.

a cotton scarf. The finishing touch may be a plain cap, a more eye-catching flat, round, black cap in Zeeland, or a military-style cap in Urk.

Marken and Volendam are two villages where traditional costume is still worn on an everyday basis. Both are fishing villages on the western shores of the IJsselmeer. Since the completion of the barrier dam cutting off the Zuiderzee from the North Sea, these villages have come to rely more on tourism than on fishing for their livelihood. The colorful costumes worn in these two villages are a major attraction for visitors.

In most areas, more women than men dress in traditional regional costumes. Older people are also more likely to wear traditional costumes on a daily basis, whereas young people usually wear modern clothes.

However, clogs, or *klompen* (KLOM-pehn), are a different matter. Like windmills and tulips, clogs are a universally recognized symbol of the Netherlands. They are still widely used by ordinary Dutch people, both men and women, when engaged in wet and dirty work. When modern dress is exchanged for traditional costume, clogs may be replaced by black leather shoes that often come with silver buckles.

FABRIC OF ALL STRIPES

Chintz is a fabric made of cotton and printed in many colors. In the seventeenth century, the Dutch East India Company imported large amounts of this fabric, which became an important part of traditional dress.

Chintz is a popular fabric even today. At Staphorst, for example, women still wear chintz bodices with large collars decorated with painted flowers above their black- or blue-striped skirts.

Striped patterns are also common elsewhere. In Volendam, traditional fashion calls for a black skirt with a striped apron or a striped skirt with a black apron. A shirt with a flowered design worn under a short-sleeved overblouse, generally black in color and topped with a pointed black bonnet, completes the outfit. On feast days, the black bonnet is exchanged for a tall, winged cap.

In Marken, women wear a wide skirt and black apron over a striped petticoat. In summer a red-and-white-striped blouse is worn under a vest with a print in front. The headdress is a lace-and-cotton skullcap.

FAMOUS DUTCH NATIVES (AND TRANSPLANTS)

For such a small country, the Netherlands has produced a surprisingly large number of famous people. Many other famous Europeans also migrated to the Netherlands because of war or persecution. They include Carl Linnaeus, the Swedish naturalist, and René Descartes, the French philosopher and mathematician.

Among the heroic and infamous Dutch people of the twentieth century are a young girl and a woman—Anne Frank and Mata Hari.

Anne Frank (1929–1945), originally from Germany, was a young Jewish girl who came to the Netherlands with her parents in the 1930s. She wrote a diary of her life while hiding from Nazi persecution in Amsterdam during World War II. Her family was eventually betrayed and discovered by the Nazis. Tragically, Frank died in the Bergen-Belsen concentration camp when she was only fifteen, just a few months before the end of the war. Nonetheless, The Diary of Anne Frank *continues to inspire all who live under the threat of persecution. Today the secret annex in an Amsterdam warehouse where her family hid for over two years is one of the city's most popular tourist attractions.*

Margaretha Geertruide Zelle (1876–1917) was a courtesan and professional dancer who took the professional name Mata Hari (meaning "the eye of the day"). During World War I, she acted as a double agent for both sides, spying for the French and the Germans. In 1917 she was shot by the French for being a German spy.

Dutch contributions to science have been far-ranging. Christiaan Huygens not only invented the pendulum clock in 1657 but also made major advances in the study of optics. Huygens invented the first successful balance spring for watches and is the originator of the wave theory of light.

Zacharias Janssen made the first microscope, and Antonie van Leeuwenhoek refined it. Leeuwenhoek became the first person to study microbiology by observing bacteria with a microscope. His work was instrumental in disproving the theory of spontaneous generation, which describes living things arising from nonliving matter.

In philosophy, religion, and the arts, the Netherlands is represented by several people whose works had a lasting impact on both the country and the European continent.

Thomas à Kempis, author of *The Imitation of Christ*, was a fifteenth century Augustinian monk who lived near Zwolle in Overijssel. His writings were among the most widely read religious works of his time throughout the whole of Europe.

Desiderius Erasmus, known universally as "The Prince of Humanists," was born in Rotterdam around 1466. The illegitimate son of a priest and his housekeeper, Erasmus attended a school run by the Order of the Bretheren of the Common Life—a community devoted to educating and caring for the poor—which had a large intellectual following in Europe.

Erasmus became a monk in 1488 and was ordained a priest in 1492. He studied the classics but found monastic life restrictive and became secretary to the bishop of Cambrai in 1494. This diplomatic career did not suit him, and he went to the Sorbonne University in Paris to study theology. In Paris, he first met the humanists, whose ideas were to change his life forever.

Erasmus traveled extensively. In England he met Sir Thomas More, author of Utopia, *who became his best friend. He became a professor for a few years in Louvain, Belgium, and traveled between England, Switzerland, and Italy. He made copies of early Greek New Testament manuscripts that eventually formed the basis of his publication of the Greek New Testament with his own Latin translation.*

Erasmus finally settled in Basel, Switzerland, where he published numerous books on classical authors—some Latin and many Greek—including annotated editions of their works. His influence on Reformation philosophers and theologians was enormous. He died in 1536, a great scholar mourned by the civilized world.

Hugo Grotius, the famous seventeenth-century jurist who lived in Delft, was imprisoned for life for his involvement in a religious dispute. Thanks to the resourcefulness of his wife, however, he managed to escape from prison by hiding in a case of books and went to France, where his works on international law were published. He is considered the founder of the science of international law; he was also an accomplished theologian, statesman, and poet.

BARUCH SPINOZA

Son of a Portuguese refugee, Baruch Spinoza was born in Amsterdam in 1632. He came from a family of prosperous merchants and respected members of the Dutch Jewish community.

Spinoza challenged the value of various sacred texts, saying, for example, that there was nothing in the Bible to support the view that God has no body, that angels really exist, or that the soul is immortal. He also advanced the view that the writer of the Pentateuch—the first five books of the Bible—was clearly not well read in physics.

For his views, Spinoza was expelled from Amsterdam and eventually moved to The Hague. He advocated the rational study of the Bible, especially the application of historical methods to biblical sources. He maintained that the inspiration of the Old Testament prophets applied only to moral and theological points, and that their factual beliefs were merely those current at the time. On this basis, he claimed, for example, that many miracles would eventually be rationally explained as scientific knowledge increased over the years.

INTERNET LINKS

www.theguardian.com/world/2015/apr/08/scientists-try-to-answer-why-dutch-people-are-so-tall
This article looks at a scientific study of how the country's population became the tallest in the world.

www.holland.com/us/tourism/activities/dutch-culture-1.htm
The government's tourism site explains the culture of the Dutch.

joshuaproject.net/countries/NL
Here you can find in-depth information about the ethnic demographics of the Netherlands.

"The highest activity a human being can attain is learning for understanding, because to understand is to be free."
–Baruch Spinoza

LIFESTYLE

These tall, thin traditional homes demonstrate that space is at a premium in the Netherlands.

7

PERHAPS THE MOST MEMORABLE aspect of the Dutch lifestyle is the prevalence of bicycles as a means of transportation. With many professionals opting to ride bicycles to work, commuting in the Netherlands looks very different from the urban commutes of other countries.

The Netherlands is a highly developed and forward-thinking nation. Like other nations, the country grapples with issues like health care reform and pension programs for retirees. The mixture of private plans and state-sponsored solutions has left the government of the Netherlands looking for a balance that works for all citizens.

STANDARDS OF LIVING

Since the end of World War II, the Netherlands has become one of the most successful European economies, and the Dutch people have enjoyed a steady increase in their overall standard of living.

The Dutch standard of living is comparable to that in the United States. The Dutch have 2.9 doctors per 1,000 people, whereas the Americans have 2.5. However, the health indicators of the Netherlands often surpass that of the United States. For instance, the infant mortality rate is 3 for every 1,000 live births in the Netherlands, compared with 6 in the United States. American ownership of televisions outstripped the Dutch until recently, but now they are equal, at almost 100 percent ownership.

HOME LIFE

After the devastation of World War II, the Dutch faced a critical housing shortage. They began building apartment blocks but tried to limit the buildings to four or five stories, often with large picture windows overlooking communal gardens. But demand for housing was so great that they were forced to build tower blocks. By 1968, almost half of the buildings under construction had nine stories or more. Despite their best efforts to avoid this situation, many Dutch cities were eventually encircled by huge concrete suburbs.

The greatest dream of the Dutch is to own a house with a garden. Family life at home is all important, and a lot of time and effort is spent on making homes cozy and welcoming. Since Dutch families spend a great deal of time together, a home atmosphere that is *gezellig* (gheh-ZEL-lig), meaning cozy and inviting, is greatly appreciated.

However, the main obstacle to housing has always been the lack of space. In the seventeenth century, when wealthy merchants built homes alongside the Amsterdam canals, only houses that were three windows wide were allowed, so houses were made tall, narrow, and deep. Modern townhouses still tend to be tall and narrow, with steep staircases.

Dutch houses have large windows both to let in sunlight and to allow families to see what is going on outside. Many older houses have a spy mirror, called a *spionnetje* (SPO-neh-tcheh), bracketed onto the outside of a window frame to make it easier to look out. The Dutch do not resent people looking into their homes and, until recently, seldom drew their curtains at night.

The Dutch have always been interested in small objects and in detail. Window ledges are likely to have a row of potted plants with a variety of knickknacks—strange shells, paperweights, carvings, and mementos of far-off places. Other household ornaments include prettily framed lace pictures displayed in windows and small paintings inset in front doors.

DUTCHWOMEN

Family life is so important to the Dutch that at one time hardly any married women went out to work. As late as 1960, only 3 percent of married women had a full-time job. In the past few decades, the situation has changed radically, particularly since the introduction of equal pay legislation. In 2015, 60 percent of Dutch women were engaged in paid work.

On the domestic front, there have also been many changes since the end of World War II. Until the late 1930s, a wife could not open a bank account without her husband's permission. Both men and women under thirty years of age needed their parents' consent to marry.

Social change has swept away these restrictions, although the law still prohibits one partner in a marriage from selling or renting part of their house, giving excessive gifts to other people, or signing hire-purchase agreements without the other's consent. These measures are all part of a general policy that is designed to keep the family together.

Women's rights organizations have been active in the Netherlands for the past eighty-five years. Women won the right to vote in 1919. In the 1970s, a Dutch feminist group called the Dolle Minas gained prominence in calling for greater equality. Literally "Crazy Minas" (Mina is a Dutch female name), six Dutch women in Amsterdam organized a movement to shelter battered women, called Blijf van Mijn Lijf ("blayf vahn mayn layf," Hands Off My Body) in 1975. In 1983, an amendment to the Dutch constitution prohibited discrimination on the basis of sex. The wage gap between men and women is shrinking. In 1995, Dutch women's hourly wages were 76 percent of men's; but by 2012 the figure was up to 82 percent.

An important figure in the Dutch feminist movement was Aletta Jacobs (1854—1929), the first woman doctor in the Netherlands. She opened the world's first birth control clinic in Amsterdam in 1882. When Jacobs tried to vote in 1883, the government responded by specifying that all voters must

Aside from practicing medicine and her work as an activist, Aletta Jacobs was also an inventor.

THE DOLLE MINAS

The Dolle Minas used visible tactics in their campaign for women's rights. According to Dutch politician Jet Bussemaker, "Not only was the content of [their] ideas radical but so was the form in which they were presented. The Dolle Minas became well known through their public actions in which they burned bras, cordoned off men's toilets in order to demonstrate the lack of women's facilities, and whistled at men on the street. The eyes of the world were soon on them—often even to their own surprise."

The group's bravado gained the attention of feminists in America. In 1971, famous American feminist Betty Friedan said, "Oh, I think the Dolle Minas are marvelous ... I think, they show more flair in the actions they take for the cause of the women, the full partnership with

men and the new identity of women. And then, well, as much flair as I've seen in the home, of course it is exploding worldwide ... " Naturally, the Dolle Minas were not the only Dutch women coming together in favor of equal rights in the 1970s. Man Vrouw Maatschappij (Man Woman Society, or MVW) was another such activist group. Yet MVW's tactics were not quite as radical as those of the Dolle Minas.

be male. She was a delegate to the International Congress of Women in 1916, assembled to discuss approaches to ending World War I. The Women's International League for Peace and Freedom, of which she was a founder, grew out of this congress. She campaigned against regulated prostitution and worked for shorter workdays, protective legislation for women workers, sex education, penal reform, women's suffrage, and marriage law reform.

PRIMARY SCHOOLS

Most schools in the Netherlands are run by private, often denominational, organizations, although there are some state schools. Full-time education is compulsory from ages five to sixteen. During this period, education is free, although some schools ask parents to make a financial contribution. Primary schools are for children ages four to twelve. There are no schools for children under four, although private playgroups and nurseries are popular.

Primary school is designed to prepare children for secondary school. In the first two years, children receive lessons in reading, writing, and mathematics.

Primary school students in The Hague.

About 70 percent of Dutch children attend private schools. Practically all schools, whether state or private, are coeducational.

The oldest university in the Netherlands is at Leiden, southwest of Amsterdam. It was founded by William of Orange in 1575.

When Leiden was attacked by the Spanish in 1574, the inhabitants opened the sluices and flooded the land. This made it possible for William to send gunboats to raise the siege. As a mark of his gratitude, he offered the city's inhabitants either freedom from taxes or a university. They chose the university.

In the seventeenth century, Leiden University was famous throughout Europe as a center of theology, science, and medicine. This was largely due to Herman Boerhaave, a professor of medicine, botany, and chemistry, who is credited with founding the modern system of medical instruction based on clinical, or "bedside," teaching.

Today Leiden University is one of the most respected universities in the Netherlands.

After this, the syllabus is widened to include Dutch, higher mathematics, writing, history, geography, science, and social studies. In their final year, students also learn English.

SECONDARY SCHOOLS

There are three types of secondary schools—general, pre-university, and vocational. Most students at general secondary schools do not go on to a university. After a four- or five-year course of study, they either attend one

TAKING CARE OF THE ELDERLY

The Dutch have always looked after their elderly, poor, and sick. In the seventeenth century, infirm and elderly relatives were often boarded at hofjes (HOF-yehs), institutions that are similar to the British alms houses.

Hofjes were built by wealthy families mainly to create peaceful homes in towns and cities for their aged relatives and employees. Many had well-tended gardens and were entirely surrounded by high walls to keep the street noises at bay. Hofjes frequently accommodated several people in self-contained, terraced houses in a quiet street.

Many have survived the passage of time, and a number are still in use today. There are about fifty hofjes in Amsterdam alone, some of which have been converted to house students who appreciate the tranquil surroundings.

of the many vocational secondary schools or go directly into industry, trade, or commerce.

Youngsters aiming for a place in university generally go to pre-university secondary schools. These offer a six-year course in preparation for entry into one of the country's eight universities or five *hogescholen* (HO-gheh-SGHO-len), which are equivalent to universities. All Dutch universities are financed directly by the central government, regardless of whether they are state or private organizations.

Adults, including many housewives, are increasingly interested in courses that were not previously available to them. Open Schools and the Open University have been established to cater to adult education.

CARING FOR THE SICK

Compared to many other countries, the Netherlands has excellent health care arrangements. Medical treatment financed by an insurance system is available to all citizens at reasonable prices. Prior to 2006, the Dutch medical insurance system was split. The less well-off were covered by public insurance. The better-off (about 40 percent of the population) were required to take private medical insurance. In 2006, public and private insurance were integrated when the Netherlands made sweeping reforms. Now everyone is covered by one compulsory standard health insurance program.

Despite the extensive state involvement in the provision of hospitals, most facilities are privately run on a denominational basis, although about one-fourth of the hospital beds in the country are in state institutions.

RETIREMENT

Dutch workers also contribute to a state pension program. In some industries, membership in an additional occupational system may be compulsory. The retirement age is sixty-five.

Although there have been proposals to reduce the retirement age to sixty-two or sixty-three, these plans have been dropped because of the expense involved. Another benefit for retired people, the linking of pension increases to the cost of living so that when the cost of living rises pensioners receive compensatory increments, is also under threat, again because of the cost to the state.

The problems encountered by the Netherlands with regard to health care and pensions are not unique. Like many other industrialized nations, the country has an aging population. Average life expectancy has risen from about fifty years in 1900 to around seventy-nine years for men and eighty-three years for women at present. As a result, there are now fewer people of working age to provide for an increasing number of elderly people.

Other factors also make free medical facilities more expensive: advances in medicine, which widen the range of treatments available, and changes in the major causes of death, such as the increase in cardiovascular diseases and cancer. Consequently, the Dutch welfare state is under severe financial strain and was especially affected by the world recession in the 1990s. Despite the unpopularity of such moves, many within the government, as well as other sectors of the population, realize that welfare benefits may have to be reduced in order to lighten the financial load.

THE "SMART HIGHWAY"

In 2012, Dutch artist and designer Daan Roosegaarde took a look at the highways in the Netherlands and saw an opportunity for innovation. Roosegaarde was worried about the Dutch government's decision to turn off streetlights due to budget constraints. He feared that this consequence of spending cuts could reduce drivers' visibility. Roosegaarde teamed up with an engineering firm, Hejimans, to test his solution to the problem: glow-in-the-dark paint that both marks lanes and illuminates the road. The "Smart Highway Project" underwent testing by Roosegaarde and the Hejimans team for two years before paint was applied to a 0.3-mile (500-meter) strip of highway in April 2014. Though the test patch is small, Roosegaarde has ideas for expanding the project throughout the Netherlands—and around the world.

So far the "Smart Highway Project" has attracted a lot of interest. Not all of the attention has been positive: many transportation officials want to see if Roosegaarde's paint, which is solar-powered, can stand up to Dutch winters. For his part, Roosegaarde is already thinking of ways to broaden the project to include paint that is sensitive to weather conditions, lights controlled by sensors, and more. Roosegaarde's work has earned him tech and design awards in the Netherlands and around the globe.

GETTING AROUND

The Dutch countryside is criss-crossed by numerous rivers and canals. Long before the advent of roads and railways, these waterways provided the country's first passenger transportation system. An extensive railway system was built in the second half of the nineteenth century. The twentieth century brought a comprehensive network of roads and freeways.

Since the land is so flat, there is little to prevent roads from being built totally straight. For safety reasons, however, they are constructed with gentle bends to keep drivers awake. Bridges over the waterways are more common than tunnels. Before World War II there was only one tunnel in the entire country—the Maas Tunnel in Rotterdam—but since then the number of tunnels has increased. One of the recent tunnels to be built is the

Cobbled streets can help regulate motorists' speeds.

Westerschelde Tunnel, which joins parts of the Zeeland Province. It was officially opened in March 2003. Plans to build more elaborate tunnels are in the works. For example, a double-deck, four-tube tunnel is being constructed in Maastricht. A 4.8-mile (3-kilometer) tunnel will also be built in the southern outskirts of Amsterdam.

Land is in such short supply that the various networks—canal, river, rail, and road—are all woven together to take up the least space possible. In towns, the roads are not laid out in a grid pattern. Narrow bridges over canals and winding streets often make driving difficult in medieval cities that have expanded haphazardly over the years.

In many rural towns and villages, the speed of through traffic is kept to an acceptable level by the old cobbled road surfaces. These have the same function as speed bumps in urban areas. The cobbles cause such alarming vibrations that drivers automatically slow down.

THE LAND OF THE BICYCLE

In such a small and crowded country, it is not surprising that the official policy is to encourage the use of public transportation, bicycles, and mopeds. These reduce fuel consumption and do less damage to the environment.

In crowded city centers, the bicycle is the ideal mode of transportation when it is not raining. In Utrecht and around Amsterdam's railway station, hundreds of bicycles are parked every day. There are about three times as many bicycles in the Netherlands as cars, and most major roads have bicycle paths alongside. People of all classes ride bicycles—at least one prime minister and some members of the royal family have been known to cycle to work. In towns, cyclists weave deftly in and out of traffic, ringing their bells.

PUBLIC TRANSPORTATION

Public transportation is modern and efficient and carries about one billion passengers a year. A coordinated system of buses, streetcars, and trains links all towns and cities in the country.

Amsterdam and Rotterdam have subway systems, and express trains leave most large towns and cities at frequent intervals. A unified bus and streetcar fare system efficiently divides the country into zones. The same tickets can be used on both urban and regional transportation.

INTERNET LINKS

www.access-nl.org/living-in-the-netherlands/lifestyle.aspx#
This website gives a great overview of the Dutch way of life, including public holidays and the legalities of marriage and divorce.

www.bbc.com/news/technology-27021291
This article examines the Dutch innovation of the "Smart Highway."

www.expatica.com/nl/about/culture-history/Dutch-society-and-working-culture_101736.html
"Going to the Dutch: Society and Working Culture" explores attitudes toward work in the Netherlands.

RELIGION

The St. Martin's Cathedral is also called Dom Church.

ALTHOUGH RELIGION WAS AN integral part of the formation of the Netherlands, today the Dutch are turning away from churches, mosques, and synagogues in record numbers. In fact, the majority of the Dutch identify themselves as non-religious. Yet many people in the Netherlands hold fast to the religions that shaped their nation. Religion was even one of the main causes of the Dutch revolt against Catholic Spanish rule in the sixteenth century.

Religion has always been a contentious issue in Dutch society. In fact, there is an old Dutch saying that goes, "One Dutchman, a theologian; two Dutchmen, a church; three Dutchmen, a schism."

THE ARRIVAL OF CHRISTIANITY

Christianity came to the Netherlands in 690 CE when an Anglo-Saxon priest named Willibrord converted the people of the region to Christianity. He also built the two churches of Saint Salvator and Saint Martin in Utrecht. When these were destroyed by fire, the cathedral in Utrecht was built between 1254 and 1517 on the site of the seventh-century churches. In the Middle Ages, Utrecht was the religious center of the northern provinces.

PROTESTANTS

Until 2004, there were two main reformed churches. The Reformed Church of the Netherlands (Nederlands Hervormde Kerk, or NHK) dated back to 1619 and had about three million members in the early 2000s. The Reformed Churches in the Netherlands (Gereformeerd Kerken in Nederland, or GKN) was founded in 1892 and had about a million members prior to 2004. GKN members were more orthodox and conservative. This group was stronger in rural areas and was traditionally working class. The NHK, on the other hand, had more liberal attitudes on social issues and was more vulnerable to the modern trend toward secularization.

In May 2004, the NHK, GKN, and the Evangelical Lutheran Church in the Kingdom of the Netherlands joined together to form the Protestant Church in the Netherlands (PKN). The merger was finalized after almost two decades of negotiations between the churches. The distinct personalities of the NHK and GKN made it difficult for church leaders to find common ground. As of 2015, the PKN had 2.5 million members.

A Catholic church in Apeldoorn.

CATHOLICS AND TOLERANCE

During the Middle Ages, all of Europe was Catholic, including the Netherlands. But with the spread of the Protestant Reformation in the sixteenth century, Protestant beliefs and practices, especially those of the reformer John Calvin, became firmly established in the Low Countries.

When the Netherlands was part of the Spanish Empire, dissenting Dutch were forced to be Catholics. But after the Dutch regained independence, Calvinism was adopted as the official religion. Even so, the Dutch adopted a tolerant attitude toward other religions, and interference with private worship was rare.

In public, the prohibition against Catholicism was upheld. There were no local bishops, so Dutch Catholics were governed by a papal vicar resident in Rome. In private, however, Catholics, Jews, and others were allowed to practice their beliefs. The Dutch authorities also turned a blind eye to the presence of Catholic priests, but they did not tolerate Jesuits because Jesuits vigorously promoted Spanish interests.

Cornelius Jansen lived from 1585 to 1638.

The situation changed slowly over time. The Dutch Catholic hierarchy was reestablished in 1853, and by the end of the nineteenth century, Catholics made up one-third of the population. In the 1960s, Catholics outnumbered all the Protestant groups put together. Today, according to Statistics Netherlands, 27 percent of the population belongs to the Catholic faith.

JANSENISTS AND OLD CATHOLICS

Two substantial Catholic splinter groups—the Jansenists and the Old Catholics—took root in the Netherlands in the seventeenth and nineteenth centuries, respectively, and have remained active on Dutch soil.

Jansenism was named after Cornelius Jansen, a Dutch professor of theology at the University of Louvain (in present-day Belgium). Jansenist

A Jewish synagogue in Groningen.

ideas flourished mostly in France. After a conflict with the Jesuits lasting one hundred years after Jansen's death, the sect was declared heretical by the pope. Its adherents were hunted down in France and many fled to Holland, where they could worship in peace. There are currently about twelve thousand Jansenists in the Netherlands, and they claim to have an unbroken line of bishops going back to the time of Saint Peter in Rome.

The Old Catholic Church came into being as a result of the doctrine of papal infallibility promulgated by the First Vatican Council in 1870. Many of Europe's most learned theologians and bishops did not accept this doctrine, which they said was unknown to the Church for the previous 1,800 years. They split from Rome and set up their own church—Catholic in every way except in the matter of the infallibility of the pope—and became known as the Old Catholics.

OTHER RELIGIONS

There are other religious groups to which Dutch people belong, however. According to Statistics Netherlands, Muslims make up 4 percent of the population. These are mainly accounted for by the immigrant population of Moroccans, Turks, Iraqis, Afghans, and Iranians. Hindus, Jews, Buddhists, and other denominations make up 6 percent of the population. The Jewish community is mainly concentrated in Amsterdam.

THE PILLARIZATION OF SOCIETY

"Pillarization" or *verzuilen* (ver-ZUEH-len), is an important factor in the structure of Dutch society.

PROTESTANTISM AND CALVINISM

In 1517, Martin Luther nailed his Ninety-Five Theses to the door of Wittenburg Church in Germany. This started the Protestant Reformation, which changed the face of religious practices in Europe.

Luther's protests focused on doctrinal issues and on corruption within the Catholic Church. Protestantism spread quickly to the Low Countries. By about 1530, the Anabaptists—a breakaway Protestant sect—were more numerous than the Lutherans. The Anabaptists rejected the baptism of infants in favor of adult baptism and had revolutionary views on other matters. They caused an uproar by refusing to swear allegiance to the prince or to serve in the armed forces.

With the passing of time, Calvinism, a form of Protestantism advocated by John Calvin, became the dominant Protestant sect in the Netherlands. Calvin believed that the church should have control of its own affairs and authority over its own members. He also expressed the view that a formal church was unnecessary for man's salvation—he believed that God speaks directly to man, not through the structures of the church, and freely bestows divine grace where he wishes. This does not mean, however, that the state is unnecessary. On the contrary, without it there would be anarchy.

Calvinism originated in France and spread largely because of the practice of public preaching and open-air services. By 1560, it was firmly established in the Low Countries. It appealed strongly to both the working classes and the middle classes because of its glorification of work and its emphasis on discipline. After the war of independence with Spain, Calvinist zeal became stronger, and other religions, especially Catholicism, were forced underground.

The Free University of Amsterdam was founded by a Calvinist in 1880.

The Dutch hold two principles very dear: first, the validity of their personal opinions, and second, the belief that different views should be given due respect. For this reason, a type of society founded on a number of "pillars" has developed, each representing different groups within the population. Each group is distinguished by a set of beliefs, and its members are organized independently of members of other pillars.

These pillars are, in a sense, the foundations of Dutch society, and they influence many areas of life in the Netherlands. Each pillar has its own newspapers, schools, trade unions, hospitals, soccer clubs, and even universities—the Protestant Free University of Amsterdam and the Radboud University of Nijmegen are two prime examples. When broadcasting started in the 1920s, there were radio stations run by the Protestant, Catholic, Socialist, and other pillars. Even today the Dutch watch television channels that are still sponsored by the same organizations.

At present there are three main pillars—Protestant, Catholic, and a third pillar that encompasses a number of neutral groups. Others may focus on a specific political viewpoint. However, now that the population is relatively secular, pillarization is less widespread.

PILLARIZATION AFTER WAR

The privations of World War II and the pressures of modern society have considerably altered the Dutch outlook on life. Perhaps the biggest change has resulted from the decline in the number of churchgoers and the increase in the number of agnostics.

In the past, the pillars helped maintain a stable, though perhaps inward-looking, society. In the last forty years, however, the pillarization system has declined with loosening religious ties.

USING CHURCHES

As more and more people in the Netherlands identify themselves as non-religious, churches and other places of worship are beginning to close, or be used for other purposes. The Wall Street Journal *reported on one such church in a 2015 story. The former church is now an indoor skate park.*

In the 1990s, the divisions within society represented by the pillars were seen as much less important, especially in the eyes of the younger generation. Intermarriage between people of different faiths is common, and even the religion-based political parties have started to merge. The Protestant and Catholic parties united in the 1960s to form the Christian Democratic Appeal, which now dominates the political center ground. In the cities and to some extent in the countryside, the division of society into rigid sectors has almost disappeared.

INTERNET LINKS

www.bbc.com/news/world-europe-14417362
The BBC reports on new interpretations of Christianity in the Netherlands in an article called "Dutch Rethink Christianity for a Doubtful World."

faculty.history.wisc.edu/sommerville/351/351-082.htm
In this article, University of Wisconsin professor J. P. Sommerville traces the evolution of early Dutch religions.

www.pewforum.org/2015/04/02/religious-projection-table
The Pew Research Center predicts the religious makeup of countries around the world, including the Netherlands, through 2050.

This 1672 map of Nieuw Amsterdam shows how Dutch place names (and words) traveled the globe with Dutch explorers.

9

DUTCH IS CONSIDERED TO BE A language with fairly straightforward grammatical rules, which has perhaps contributed to its prevalence in other nations. The language is spoken beyond the borders of the Netherlands: in Suriname, a former colony of the Netherlands, Dutch is the official language. Dutch words have made their way into other languages, too.

Dutch is not the only language spoken in the Netherlands, though. Newcomers to the country have brought a chorus of languages from their homelands, and English is spoken around the country by a surprising number of Dutch citizens. The majority of the Dutch report fluency in English.

ENGLISH WORDS, DUTCH ROOTS

Dutch expertise in sailing and navigation has also led to many Dutch nautical terms finding their way into the English language, such as "smuggler" and "reef." The Dutch also contributed words to American English—these include "boss," "waffle," "cookie," "duffle," and "snoop." Dutch immigrants in the Cape Province in South Africa contributed "commando" and "trek."

Dutch influence can also be seen in American place names—Harlem and Brooklyn in New York City are named after the towns of Haarlem in North Holland and Breukelen in Utrecht. This is a side effect of New York City being formerly called Nieuw Amsterdam by its early Dutch settlers.

The Dutch language is spoken all over the Netherlands, in addition to northern Belgium, where it is known as Flemish. It is also used along with native languages in the Netherlands Antilles in the Caribbean. Afrikaans, a language spoken widely by the white population in South Africa, is derived from the Dutch language.

PRONUNCIATION

Although a simplified, phonetic spelling was introduced after World War II, Dutch pronunciation can still be confusing. Written Dutch looks difficult until one becomes familiar with the spelling conventions. For example, the combination *ij* is considered a single letter in Dutch and is pronounced "eye." Words beginning with *ij* capitalize both letters, as in IJsselmeer. In the phone directory, *ij* is listed after the letter *y*.

The letters *ui*, as in *huis*, are pronounced like *ou* in "house." The letter *g* is pronounced *kh*, a guttural sound rather like the Scottish word *loch*. The name of the famous Dutch painter Van Gogh is pronounced "van go" in the United States, "van goff" in Great Britain, and "van khoch" in Dutch. The letters *jk* are pronounced without the *j* sound but with a *y* sound—for example, the word *dijk* is pronounced "dayk."

DIALECTS AND OTHER LANGUAGES

The Netherlands has a large number of dialects, generally named after the regions in which they are spoken. The regions of Veluwe, Groningen, Drenthe, and Gelderland all have their own dialects. Frankish is spoken on the German border, and dialects of Vlaams (or Flemish) are found in the south in Brabant and Limburg. Frisian, spoken in Friesland Province, is classified as a distinct language. It is not understood by ordinary Dutch-speaking people.

Standard Dutch is known as *Algemeen Beschaafd Nederlands* (AHL-heh-main Behs-SHAAHFT NAY-der-lands), meaning General Cultural Dutch. It is taught in schools and used for official purposes.

Since the Netherlands is surrounded by larger European countries, most Dutch people learn a second language. English is the most popular, followed by German and French. There is a remarkably high standard of spoken English, especially in the towns and cities. Nowadays, the use of English words in Dutch is much greater than any other language. Many French words entered the language during the reign of Napoleon. Still prevalent today is the use of the French expression for "please," *s'il vous plait*, either spelled out or abbreviated as *svp* on public signs.

FORMS OF ADDRESS

The Dutch are generally informal in their dealings with one another, both in speech and in writing. Although an aristocracy still exists, it has integrated well with the rest of the population. Thus, in Great Britain, for example, one would use a title such as "Sir" or "Lord" when addressing a titled person, but in the Netherlands this is not usually so, except on the most formal of occasions.

When writing to a Dutch person, the address on the envelope includes the Dutch equivalent of "Mr." or "Mrs." "Mr." is written as *Hr*, standing for *Heer*—short for *Mijnheer* (mehn-NEER). For "Mrs.," the Dutch write *Mw* or *Mevr*, standing for *Mevrouw* (mehv-FRAOW). "Miss" is *Mejuffrouw* (may-YOU-fraow) and is abbreviated to *Mej*. Thus, a letter to a Mr. and Mrs. Jansen would be addressed to *Hr & Mw Jansen*. A letter to Hr Jansen's daughter, Marieke, would be addressed to *Mej M. Jansen*.

If the precise details of a person's titles and qualifications are not known to the writer, the letters "SSTT" are sometimes added after the name of the addressee. These stand for *Salvis Titulis*, a Latin term, and indicate that the sender does not know what title or form of address to use but means no disrespect by omitting the title.

When meeting other people for the first time, the Dutch address them as *Mijnheer* or *Mevrouw*, just as we might say, "Hello, Mr. Smith." Generally, however, the Dutch prefer to be informal and quickly move on to using first names.

RADIO AND TELEVISION

Radio broadcasting started in the Netherlands in 1928. Unlike radio stations elsewhere in Europe, programming is left to private enterprise, with little or no government interference. There are five national radio stations broadcasting on AM or FM. Radio 3 is a pop station and Radio 4 transmits only classical music. The others feature varied content.

Radio Nederland, an independent station, is the Dutch equivalent of the Voice of America. It transmits programs in Dutch, English, Spanish,

In 2015, the New York Times *reported that "in the Netherlands, some 75 percent of all books produced are translations, according to 2013 statistics—and about 10 percent of all general interest books sold are original, English-language versions." The Dutch have even gained a reputation for their English fluency. Scholars have a number of theories about how the Dutch have mastered the English language, and their conclusions might surprise you. Many researchers feel that it is English immersion outside of school that has led the Dutch—and many young Dutch students in particular—to achieve English fluency. They cite the time young people spend listening to English-language music and watching movies in English with Dutch subtitles. Neighboring countries often broadcast movies dubbed over in their native language, and it seems that this could be a missed learning opportunity. No matter the reason, a large percentage of the Dutch spend their leisure time reading books in English, no translation necessary.*

Portuguese, Indonesian, Arabic, French, Sranan Tongo (for Suriname), and Papiamento (for the Netherlands Antilles).

Television broadcasting dates from 1951, and there are currently three national channels. Dutch viewers are also able to watch programs from several surrounding countries, especially neighboring England, Germany, and Belgium. Most households are connected to the cable network, and satellite television is also gaining in popularity.

Advertising generates income for both radio and television stations. The commercials are subject to a government code to ensure they are in good taste and conform to legal requirements. Some advertising is restricted. Alcoholic drinks, for example, may only be advertised in limited circumstances, and tobacco advertising is totally prohibited.

FREEDOM OF SPEECH

Freedom of speech is one of the cornerstones of Dutch democracy, and for this reason, the government encourages the expression of a wide range of opinions in the press and broadcasting organizations.

Newspapers enjoy various tax and postal concessions, and broadcasting organizations receive financial aid from the sale of licenses. A Press Fund was set up in 1974 to assist newspapers and news weeklies to receive financial support from the government.

Nearly all newspapers are sold by subscription and are delivered directly to people's homes. Just a few are sold in roadside stands and supermarkets. Most national papers are morning papers.

COMMON DUTCH PHRASES

To greet someone, the Dutch say "hallo," similar to the English "hello." Depending on the time of day, one would then say, "*Goede morgen*" (HOO-deh MOR-hen, good morning), or "*Goede middag*" (HOO-deh MEE-dagh, good afternoon), or "*Goede avond*" (HOO-deh AH-vunt, good evening). A visitor might also hear "*Goeie morgen*" (HOO-yeh MOR-hen), "*Goeie middag*," or "*Goeie avond*," which are more colloquial ways of saying these greetings. "*Aangenaam*" (AHN-heh-nam) means "pleased to meet you."

To say good-bye, one could say, "*Tot volgende keer*" (toht vohl-hen-deh-KAYR, see you next time). "*Dag*" (dach) also means good-bye, and "*Tot ziens*" (toht-SEENS) means "See you."

INTERNET LINKS

www.britannica.com/topic/Frisian-language
The *Encyclopedia Britannica* gives background about the Frisian language.

www.learndutch.org
A free online language course teaches Dutch fluency (or at least basic vocabulary).

www.omniglot.com/writing/dutch.htm
Explore an overview of the Dutch language, audio clips, pronunciation tips, and useful links on Omniglot's "Dutch (Nederlands)" page.

ARTS

The EYE Film Institute opened in 2012.

10

W HEN IT COMES TO THE ARTS, the Dutch shine. Some of the most famous painters in the history of art have hailed from the Netherlands. These giants of the field include old Dutch masters and modern artists. The Dutch are also celebrated in music, dance, and architecture. University programs like that of the Design Academy Eindhoven and the Royal Academy of Art in The Hague routinely produce the biggest names in graphic design and furniture design. In old cities like Amsterdam, classic architecture blends with cutting edge buildings and museums.

Old Dutch masters such as Rembrandt and Vermeer have long enjoyed international fame, as have Van Gogh and Mondrian. Meanwhile, on a more popular level, M. C. Escher has achieved a cult following for his intriguing drawings and engravings, which combine science and art.

ARTS FUNDING

The government actively supports art and artists by subsidizing literary and artistic magazines, theater workshops, and other experimental projects. Municipal councils often commission artists to produce works for public buildings. Similarly, ballet, modern dance, and music receive substantial official sponsorship.

Frans Hals painted *Jester with a Lute* between 1620 and 1625.

These policies have contributed to a resurgence of artistic activity in the past few years. Amsterdam is now one of the leading artistic centers in Europe, with thousands of painters, sculptors, musicians, and writers coming together to create an atmosphere similar to that of Paris in the 1930s.

DUTCH MASTERS

The artistic reputation of the Dutch is primarily built on the genius of the great masters of the seventeenth century—Rembrandt van Rijn, Frans Hals, Jan Vermeer, and Jan Steen—but in addition to these, the Netherlands has produced a host of great painters.

The arts of the Golden Age were primarily intended to decorate the homes and celebrate the achievements of rich merchants. As a result, the subjects painted were mainly secular and provided later generations with a remarkable record of the daily life of the times. Dutch artists excelled in detailed portraits of daily life, domestic interiors, guild portraits, and landscapes to decorate the houses of the wealthy.

Jan Vermeer painted quiet interior scenes with painstaking precision. Despite the simplicity of his subject matter, his use of light, vivid tones, geometry, and composition raised his portrayal of domestic scenes to the level of masterpieces. Paintings such as *The Kitchen Maid*, *The Young Woman Reading a Letter*, and *Girl with a Pearl Earring* are examples of his choice of subjects and skill.

Jan Steen is noted for his cheerful pictures, often of inn scenes, executed with verve and delicacy and painted very much from life. Steen was an innkeeper because he could not make a living from painting. In contrast, Jacob van Ruisdael created dark, romantic landscapes with somber clouds, gnarled forests, and ruined castles.

Group portraits of guild members, civic guards, surgeons, almshouse regents, and other dignitaries are also characteristic of this period. These

VINCENT VAN GOGH

Vincent Van Gogh was born near Breda, North Brabant, in 1853. His first pictures were painted in somber colors, but after moving to Paris in 1886 and coming into contact with the impressionists, his pictures became more luminous and colorful.

A couple of years later, he went to Arles in southern France to shut himself away from the world and to paint undisturbed. But he was desperately lonely and under great strain, mainly because he was trying to make a living from painting to repay his brother, who was supporting him. He painted frenzied wheat fields and tormented olive and cypress trees twisted by the mistral (mis-TRAAHL), a wind that blows across southern France. From time to time, he lapsed into temporary insanity and had to be hospitalized, but continued painting during lucid intervals. Tragically, in 1890, he took his own life.

Van Gogh used color and form to convey what he felt about the scene before his eyes. He distorted shapes and used color in unusual ways. He frequently applied paint in broad brushstrokes, laying on the color thickly.

During his lifetime, Van Gogh only managed to sell one painting, but over a hundred years after his death, his painting The Sunflowers *was sold for $53 million.*

were the specialty of two outstanding figures—Frans Hals and Rembrandt van Rijn. Frans Hals is remembered for magnificent canvases such as *The Banquet of the Officers of the St. George Militia of Haarlem*, as well as for smaller portraits like that of *The Jolly Toper*.

Whether he was painting individuals or groups, Rembrandt—undoubtedly one of the world's greatest artists—emphasized the human element in his portraits. In later life, he developed a taste for strong contrasts between light and shade, and painted such dramatic scenes as *The Night Watch* and *The Anatomy Lesson of Dr. Tulp*. He is also famous for his self-portraits, which show him in his youth, at the height of his career as a successful master, and later moving into a sad old age.

Most of the Netherlands' artistic treasures from this age are contained in the Rijksmuseum in Amsterdam, the Mauritshuis in The Hague, and the Frans Hals Museum in Haarlem.

Artists from before the Golden Age include Jan van Eyck, who founded the Flemish school in the fifteenth century, Hieronymus Bosch, known for his fantastic religious paintings, and Pieter Bruegel the Elder, who excelled in everyday scenes.

MODERN ARTISTS

Willem de Kooning, a Dutchman who emigrated to the United States, was famous for his abstract expressionist paintings. De Kooning's work influenced an entire generation of painters. His work is part of major collections in museums around the world. Other modern painters and sculptors include Wessel Couzijn, Carel Visser, Jan Dibbets, Ad Dekkers, Ger van Elk, and Martha Röling.

Willem de Kooning (*right*) and his wife Elaine (*left*), who was also an important abstract expressionist.

MOVIES AND PLAYS

The Dutch are not enthusiastic theater-goers, and theater is subsidized to ensure its survival. Most plays performed are translations of English, French, or German works. Similarly most movies shown are from the United States, France, Great Britain, and Germany, with Dutch subtitles.

Both forms of entertainment suffer from a language problem—a Dutch movie or play may meet with great success at home, but it is unlikely to be noticed elsewhere because Dutch is not spoken internationally. Similarly, in Dutch literature, there are many excellent writers, but their work seldom reaches an international audience. However, some younger writers are trying to overcome the language problem by writing in English.

MUSIC AND DANCE

Music plays a central part in Dutch life. There are few families in which no one plays an instrument or sings in a choir. In the country as a whole, just about every town has its own amateur orchestra, chamber music ensemble, or choral society. The big cities have their own symphony orchestras, and Amsterdam's Royal Concertgebouw Orchestra achieved worldwide fame under the baton of Bernard Haitink. Opera still plays only a small role on the cultural scene.

Dutch composers are not well known internationally. The most famous is perhaps Jan Pieterzoon Sweelinck (1562—1621), who was an organist in Amsterdam. Living composers who are recognized outside the country are Louis Andriessen and Michel van der Aa.

Modern Dutch writers include Simon Vestdijk, whose works have been translated into many languages. However, his international success has not matched his great talent.

The Royal Concertgebouw Orchestra plays a concert in Berlin, Germany, in 2010.

Unlike music, which has deep roots in Dutch society, ballet has been an established part of the Dutch cultural life for a comparatively short time. On the other hand, since World War II, modern dance forms have become extremely popular with performers and audiences alike.

MUSIC IN THE STREETS

Such is their love of music that the Dutch contrive to have it everywhere, not just in the concert hall. On a fine day, the streets and parks are alive with its sound. Street music comes from two contrasting sources—ornate barrel organs in ordinary shopping streets and melodious carillons in municipal and ecclesiastical buildings.

With their cheerful toe-tapping music and moving figures, the barrel organs entertain shoppers and passersby. They are so popular that some towns retain their own barrel organs for regular use.

The "De Adriaen" barrel organ in Lisse.

Every year in The Hague, dancers and choreographers from around the world gather to participate in the Holland Dance Festival. The festival, which took place for the first time in 1987, celebrates modern dance through performances and workshops. The festival lasts for three weeks.

Dance also plays a major role in the Holland Festival, which showcases the arts. Dance performances have been a big part of the festival since it began in 1947. The Holland Festival takes place in venues around Amsterdam. Like the Holland Dance Festival, this festival is nearly a month long.

For fans of dance music, like trance and EDM, there is a one-day festival in Spaarnwoude called Dance Valley. Featuring ten performance stages and a huge lineup of performers, Dance Valley has been bringing dance music to Spaarnwoude for over twenty years. Dance Valley is sometimes described as "the Woodstock of Dance [music]." The Netherlands also holds a variety of festivals for more traditional forms of music. It's easy to find classical, jazz, and folk music festivals, especially in the summer months. These popular music festivals are often well attended by Dutch citizens. The larger festivals draw an international crowd.

In contrast with the upbeat music of the barrel organ, the carillon with its fixed bells—sometimes as many as fifty—produces a gentler kind of music. The bells were originally activated by a clockwork mechanism, but modern carillons are generally played by a carilloneur (cah-ree-yon-NEUR) sitting at a keyboard. Carillon music enjoys such a following that there has been a school for carilloneurs at Amersfoort since 1953, and there is a carillon museum at Asten, near Eindhoven.

ARCHITECTURE

Dutch urban architecture has been famous for centuries, and in the post-war period, architects have gained a wide reputation for innovation. In recent years, Dutch town planners have developed a number of interesting solutions to the problem of housing an expanding population.

The mansions of the Damrak district in Amsterdam.

The wealthy merchant classes of the Golden Age built impressive homes, but the limited space restricted both size and design. In Amsterdam, when the city's original concentric canals were under construction, the city fathers restricted the width of the canalside houses to the width of three windows. As a result, people had to build their mansions tall and deep.

At first glance, these solid buildings appear to be identical, but a closer look reveals a wealth of detail and variety. Buildings were constructed using small bricks and faced with stone—an expensive commodity because of its scarcity in the country. The houses' most eye-catching features are the traditional Dutch gables.

FURNITURE DESIGN

With the home playing such an important part in daily life, the Dutch have a taste for fine and solid furniture. In terms of design, their furniture reached its artistic peak at the end of the sixteenth century.

Dutch Renaissance wardrobes are among the most famous items of the period. They had four doors, were topped with a cornice sometimes carved with plants, and sat on a wide plinth. Decorative touches included intricate carvings, featuring lions, caryatids, scrolls, and various geometrical designs. Regional variations include the Zeeland wardrobe, which was wider than it was high, while Frisian wardrobes had only two doors.

In the seventeenth and eighteenth centuries, there was a flowering of marquetry and inlay work. Ebony, tortoiseshell, ivory, and metals were inlaid into desks, writing tables, cabinets, and drawers.

Today, Dutch furniture design is unique in its innovative approach to style and function, taking into consideration smaller spaces of modern homes. Furniture such as armchairs and work desks combine practical use and comfort with an understated contemporary elegance.

INTERNET LINKS

www.cooperhewitt.org/tag/dutch
The Cooper Hewitt (Smithsonian Design Museum) showcases Dutch designers.

www.theguardian.com/music/2012/jun/11/sounds-netherlands-history-dutch-pop
The *Guardian* includes audio and video in their roundup called "A History of Dutch Pop in 10 Songs."

www.moma.org/collection/artists/4057
The Museum of Modern Art profiles Piet Mondrian.

www.vangoghmuseum.nl/en
This link leads to the official site of the Netherlands' Van Gogh Museum.

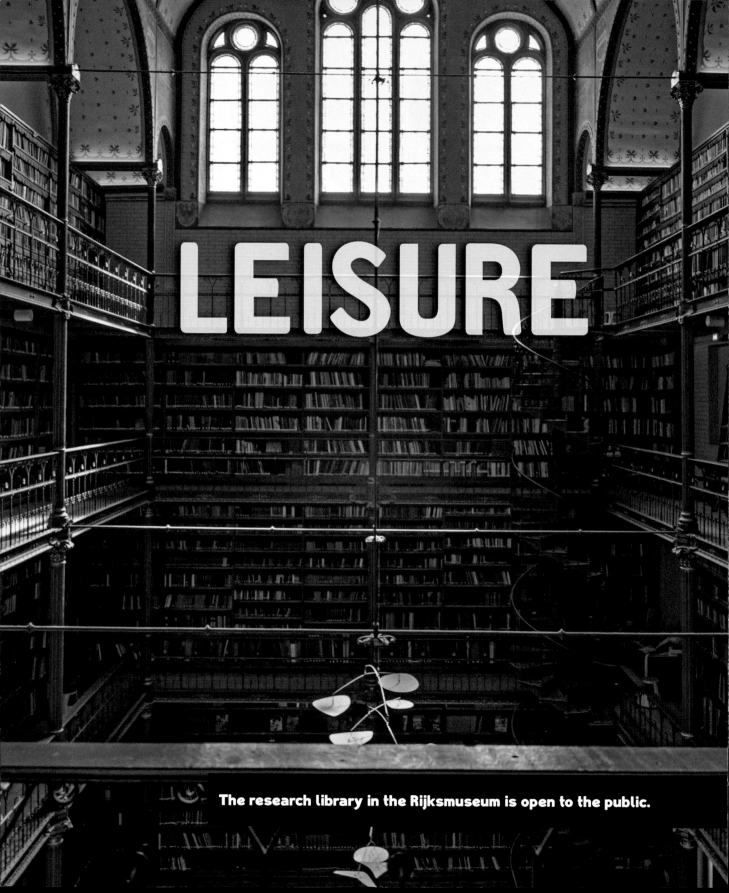

LEISURE

The research library in the Rijksmuseum is open to the public.

THE DUTCH ENJOY ONE OF THE shortest workweeks in the world, with many Dutch workers opting to work just four days each week. With more leisure time, the people of the Netherlands have relaxing down to a science. Despite more flexibility at the office, most Dutch citizens choose to stay close to home in their down time. Playing sports, especially regional inventions, and spending time with family rate high on the list of Dutch leisure activities.

In the mid 1950s, a nationwide survey found that the Dutch spent most of their spare time at home. Although there is increased participation in sporting activities, led by an interest in soccer, the Dutch are still a home-loving people today.

HOW THE DUTCH UNWIND

Traditionally, the Dutch tend not to indulge in entertainment outside the home. Long, cold, winter evenings make a cozy home seem especially inviting. There is little incentive to venture out, and a comfortable evening at home with the newspaper, a good book, or an entertaining program on television is hard to beat.

After getting home from work, people sometimes relax with wine, beer, or a *jenever* (jeh-NAY-ver)—a small glass of Dutch gin, drunk chilled and undiluted, but not on ice. After the evening meal the family settles down to enjoy time together.

Younger people are likely to be out and about during the evenings, visiting friends, dancing at a nightclub, and enjoying themselves in a lively fashion. For their parents, the chances are that catching up on the news is the first priority. Some Dutch newspapers are evening editions, so those staying in may spend a part of the evening going through the news. Holland has one of the highest newspaper subscriptions per capita in the world.

The Dutch are great readers in other ways, too. Public libraries lend millions of books per year. So many people are multilingual that bookshops carry large stocks of English, French, and German books. Foreign bestsellers are likely to be translated into Dutch and published in paperback editions.

Television is another great draw, and most households have their own set. There are plenty of channels to choose from. Many television programs are broadcast from Great Britain, the United States, and Germany, and there is easy access to programs from neighboring European countries. However good the entertainment, many families still spend the evening just chatting,

The Amsterdam Boat Show includes hands-on activities for children.

listening to music, or making music together. Friends may also drop in for a chat over a cup of tea or coffee or perhaps some cake.

Weekend activities might include a shopping expedition on Saturday and a leisure excursion on Sunday. Because going to church is no longer very common, families have outings together—a walk or a visit to a local event or a nearby museum. Weekends are also a good time to meet up with friends and relatives and have a relaxing day.

Sports are gradually playing a more important part in Dutch life compared to a century ago, when only 0.6 percent of the population took part in sports. Today there are facilities for around sixty different sports. Nearly half the population older than fifteen participate in sports every week. There are also several local and international exhibitions that are held frequently, such as the Amsterdam Boat Show and the Bicycle Show, where people can find out more about the latest models for their favorite recreation.

The North Sea coastline is a great place for families to unwind.

NATIONAL SPORTS

The Dutch have long been passionate about soccer, which they call *voetbal* (VOOT-bahl). The Royal Netherlands Football Association has almost one million members. In the 1970s, the Dutch soccer player Johan Cruyff was among the most famous and talented players in the world. A number of Dutch teams rank among the best in the world—Ajax Amsterdam, Feyenoord Rotterdam, and PSV in Eindhoven have a tremendous national as well as local following. Tennis, with five hundred thousand players belonging to various clubs, is the second-largest organized sport in the country.

The Dutch have been walking and cycling—all activities with their roots deep in the Dutch landscape and history—far longer than they have been

Some ice skating rinks are in close proximity to famous landmarks, like this one in front of the Rijksmuseum.

KORFBAL

Korfbal (spelled korfball in English) is a sport similar to basketball. It is notable because of its coed teams. The sport was invented by Nico Broekhuysen in 1902. Broekhuysen was a teacher who visited Sweden as part of a program to introduce new physical education requirements in schools. He adapted a sport he saw there, and it became popular throughout the Netherlands. Today, korfball is played around the world. The sport is governed by the International Korfball Federation (IKF).

playing soccer and tennis. In summer, the Dutch countryside offers many opportunities for swimming, sailing, and water-skiing in specially created watersports areas, often in newly reclaimed parts of the land or on the shores of the Netherlands' numerous lakes. Towns and cities have indoor and outdoor pools, and the 150-mile (240-kilometer) coastline along the North Sea caters to those who seek open spaces.

Once the sport of the privileged, boating and sailing is brought within the reach of most of the population through clubs and sailing schools. Visiting boat shows also fuel the interests of boating enthusiasts.

ICE SKATING

The Dutch are great skating devotees, and nearly all Dutch children learn to skate. During an exceptionally cold winter—about once every five or six years—the canals freeze over, and adults and children collect their skates and take to the ice. Fortified by hot chocolate sold on wayside stalls, they skate on the frozen canals across the polders and around the towns. However, frozen canals are now becoming more rare, thought to be due to global warming caused by the increase in greenhouse gases, such as carbon dioxide, in the atmosphere.

When canal skating is not possible, skating enthusiasts have to make do with the many artificial ice rinks that have been built in recent years, which are also used for speed skating, figure skating, and ice hockey.

Fierljeppen requires a pole, a canal, and a lot of skill.

UNIQUE ATHLETICS

Several quaint local sports have survived to the present day. The most widely known is *fierljeppen* (feerl-YEP-pen), or vaulting over canals or wide ditches with the help of a long pole. It is a Friesland specialty and at one time was the farmers' only means of crossing ditches and waterlogged land.

The Ringrijden (RING-ray-den) is held at Middelburg in Zeeland Province each August. Riders on horseback aim a lance at small, suspended rings.

INTERNATIONAL TRAVEL

The Dutch enjoy the warmth and sunshine of the Mediterranean countries, so many of them head for Spain or Italy for their vacations. With rising incomes, more Dutch people can now afford to vacation abroad. Inexpensive package tours have made dreams of sunshine-filled days come true.

Germany, France, Belgium, Luxembourg, and Great Britain also receive their share of Dutch visitors. The number of vacationers who drive their cars abroad on road trips has also increased, especially when going to a neighboring country.

DOMESTIC TRAVEL

For every Dutch family that vacations abroad, there are just as many who stay at home. Many go on camping trips where they can sail or swim, relax on the beach, and take life easy.

Cycling tours are popular, and it is common to meet a family pedaling through the woods or over coastal dunes. The land is crisscrossed by bicycle paths. Many pass through pretty countryside and make cycling a pleasure. But the sun does not always shine, and cyclists frequently have to struggle against strong winds and rain blowing across the polders.

Like cycling, walking is also well organized and is served by several clubs. Real enthusiasts, of which there are many thousands, young and old, may take part in the annual four-day walking event in Nijmegen. This takes place in July and involves hikes of up to 30 miles (48 km).

Another walking possibility is *wadlopen* (WAHD-loh-pen), or mud-walking on the mud flats from the mainland across the Waddenzee to the West Frisian islands. This popular walk is possible only at low tide.

The Ringrijden takes place on increasingly difficult courses as the tournament progresses.

INTERNET LINKS

www.bbc.com/sport/football/teams/netherlands
This website gives breaking news about the Netherlands' soccer team.

www.frommers.com/destinations/the-netherlands/252476
Frommer's selects the Netherlands' best museums.

www.nytimes.com/2012/07/19/world/europe/little-known-dutch-sports-experience-a-revival.html
The *New York Times* describes renewed interest in canal jumping.

FESTIVALS

On King's Day, many people wear orange to celebrate the king's lineage, the House of Orange.

12

I T SEEMS THAT IN THE NETHERLANDS, there is a festival to commemorate each holiday, to mark each royal milestone, and to show the world the unique Dutch identity. Festivals range from outdoor musical performances to the annual flower parades, which feature massive floats covered in blooms. There's a festival to be found each season, and the Dutch enjoy coming together to revel. These festivals attract tourists from around the world, bringing revenue to Dutch cities.

THE KING'S BIRTHDAY

The King's Official Birthday—Koningsdag (koh-nings-dagh)—on April 27 is a public holiday. The holiday is also known as King's Day. It is a major event in the Netherlands. Citizens dressed in orange gather to demonstrate their love of the king—and to have a good time. There are concerts, parties, and even large-scale flea markets. The royal family travels to several cities to join in the celebration.

Prior to Queen Beatrix's abdication, the Dutch celebrated her birthday during a celebration called Koninginnedag (koh-nee-HEE-neh-dagh) on April 30. Queen's Day was not always celebrated on the same

King Willem-Alexander addressed Dutch citizens on his first King's Day, saying, "It was unforgettable … heartfelt thanks to you from me and my family." Many festival-goers share the feeling that the word "unforgettable" captures the experience of attending the unique celebrations of the Netherlands.

King Willem-Alexander (*right*) and Queen Maxima (*left*) prepare to lay a wreath on a war memorial in 2015.

date. Queen Wilhelmina celebrated her first birthday as queen in 1891 on her real birthday—August 31. Since this day also fell at the end of the school summer vacations, it soon became a holiday for all Dutch schoolchildren.

Wilhelmina was succeeded by Juliana in 1948, and Koninginnedag was moved to the new queen's real birthday—April 30. In the meantime, the floral tributes that had been offered initially to her grandmother, Queen Emma, on her birthday on August 2, had grown first into a grand parade and then into a national celebration on Queen Juliana's birthday. It also became the tradition for everyone to be given a day off work.

In 1980 when Queen Beatrix succeeded to the throne on April 30, it was decided that this day—also her mother's birthday—be retained as the monarch's official birthday and a public holiday for all citizens. One reason was because the weather on January 31, Queen Beatrix's actual birthday, was often unsuitable for outdoor celebrations.

REMEMBRANCE DAY AND LIBERATION DAY

Remembrance Day on May 4 commemorates those who died during World War II. Although this is not a public holiday, the whole country observes a two-minute moment of silence at 8 p.m.—trains, trams, and all road traffic comes to a stop, and the whole country is at a standstill.

Just before 8 p.m., King Willem-Alexander lays a wreath at the War Memorial in the Dam in front of the Royal Palace in Amsterdam. The prime minister and senior members of the government are also present.

Liberation Day on May 5 commemorates the end of the German occupation period in 1945. It is a national holiday only every five years. However, civil servants have Liberation Day as a holiday every year.

CARNIVAL SEASON

February is carnival time, especially in southern provinces such as Limburg, which are largely Catholic. The seven weeks leading up to the start of Lent constitute the carnival season.

The tradition goes back to the fifteenth century, when the south was ruled by the dukes of Burgundy and the people of the region acquired a taste for open-air theaters, banquets, and riotous celebrations. Major carnivals are held seven weeks before Easter. Some draw participants and spectators from far and wide; some are almost private affairs of interest only to residents of the town staging the event. Preparations for carnivals start many weeks in advance, and there is a great feeling of community spirit. Bands practice, songs are composed, processional floats are designed, shops are decorated, and gatherings enliven the cold winter days and nights.

Carnival is known for elaborate costumes.

On Carnival Day itself, the town resounds with music—in the street, in restaurants, and in the procession. Thousands of visitors throng the sidewalks to see the fun, which often verges on the outrageous. Music, dance, and colorful parades are a feature of Carnival Day. At the stroke of midnight, the celebrations stop and Lent begins. The contrast of the carnival feasting and merriment with the austerity of the Lenten fasting period highlights the conflict between the demands of the material world and the spiritual life.

EASTER

The Easter and Whitsun holidays usually fall in March or April each year. Devout Christians attend a church service on Good Friday evening and another on Easter Sunday.

On Easter, children play games with Easter eggs. Parents hide chocolate eggs and candies all over the house and garden, and children have a merry time hunting for them. In another Dutch game called *eiertikken* (eh-yer-TIK-ken), children bump their decorated eggs together to see whose will break first.

CHRISTMAS AND NEW YEAR

The Christmas season runs from the feast of St. Nicholas on December 5 to Christmas Day. Until quite recently, the celebrations focused solely on Saint Nicholas, or Sinterklaas (SIN-ter-klahs), as the Dutch call him.

According to tradition, Sinterklaas leaves Spain at the end of November, on a boat with his Moorish attendant, Zwarte Piet (ZWAR-teh peet, or Black Pete). When Sinterklaas and Zwarte Piet arrive in Amsterdam, they are welcomed with great ceremony by the mayor. Then, seated on a white horse and dressed as a bishop, Sinterklaas leads a procession through the city.

Zwarte Piet distributes sweets to the children in the crowd who have been good. He also carries a cane to punish children who have been naughty, but, of course, he never uses it.

Interestingly, the American Santa Claus was born out of the Dutch Sinterklaas. Americans learned about Sinterklaas from Dutch immigrants who brought their Christmas traditions to the United States. Since the Dutch pronunciation of Sinterklaas was difficult to grasp, in time he became known as Santa Claus. An American poet, Clement C. Moore, created the figure of a jolly, fat man dressed in furs in "A Visit from St. Nicholas", and Santa Claus then became known to the rest of the world.

On the eve of St. Nicholas's Day, December 5, families gather together. The children are usually very excited, knowing that Sinterklaas has arrived in the Netherlands and will be coming to their homes. They put their shoes on the fireplace at night for their presents and also add a little gift for Sinterklaas's horse, such as a carrot or some water. During the night, small gifts are put into the shoes, and the carrots and water disappear.

Adults also join in the fun by giving each other small, sometimes humorous presents, and writing amusing poems about each other. Traditionally, the verses are supposed to be anonymous, but they are usually written by the donor of the present. It is now possible to buy ready-written poems or even hire a poet to write them. The poems are not always flattering—they tease people by referring to habits that others find annoying. But all this is lighthearted humor and taken in good spirits.

THE ZWARTE PIET CONTROVERSY

In the contemporary Netherlands, the representation of Sinterklaas's sidekick Zwarte Piet has caused rising tension. Usually, the person playing him is white but wears black face paint. Today, many people consider this upsetting and disrespectful. In 2014, protests broke out during the annual ceremony welcoming Sinterklaas and Zwarte Piet to the city of Gouda. These protests led to ninety arrests, and those arrested included both the protesters and men and women in favor of Zwarte Piet. Critics say that Zwarte Piet is racist, and that it is unacceptable to endorse the practice of blackface. These critics point out that when white people employ blackface, it is a divisive act that brings back memories of the brutality of the colonial era. Those in favor of Zwarte Piet believe that the character has nothing to do with race. They feel that painting their faces black represents the soot on Piet's face from climbing down a chimney. Even the United Nations has entered the debate, condemning the practice and calling for the end of Zwarte Piet.

Christmas Day is a quiet occasion, with a family feast featuring meat, fish, or game such as hare and venison. Traditionally, no gifts are exchanged during Christmas, although some families may do so following the American tradition.

New Year's Eve is an occasion for partying and celebrations. Church bells ring, fireworks displays take place, and in the harbors ships sound their sirens to welcome the New Year.

CULTURAL FESTIVALS AND FLORAL PARADES

The Netherlands enjoys a wide variety of festive events involving flowers, cheese, windmills, music, kite flying, and many other activities. Some are staged as one-time events, but many, like the Holland Festival, take place on an annual basis. A few have long histories, but most have been created since World War II.

The Holland Festival is held every year in June and July and is an officially sponsored event. It features plays, concerts, ballet, music, dance, and exhibitions, and draws leading international artists and groups, as well as lesser-known names from home and abroad. A deliberately contemporary program distinguishes it from other European festivals.

The first Holland Festival was held in 1947, and the event came to be rated as one of the best of its kind in Europe. But living up to that kind of success is a big problem, and some people feel that standards have dropped in recent years.

The North Sea Jazz Festival, held in The Hague every July, is growing more and more popular. It has been called the best jazz festival outside the United States. Utrecht has a Festival of Old Music covering music from the Middle Ages to the romantic era.

Flower festivals continue to thrive and are always popular, as are the numerous flower parades. They are held all over the country but are mostly local affairs. August and September are the best flower-festival months, and cities and towns are filled with colorful floats, extravagantly decorated with thousands of blooms. One festival specializes in vegetables and harvest products and is especially attractive.

This amazing float is made of blooming flowers.

Processions of floats wend their way through the streets in a blaze of color, accompanied by bands, cheerleaders, and trick cyclists. Aalsmeer claims to have the largest festival. Its floats go on show on a Friday, the parade is held on a Saturday, and the floats can be viewed again on Sunday. The oldest flower pageant is held at Zundert near the border with Belgium. This pageant draws many flower lovers, who come to see the best display of dahlias in the country.

Other interesting regional festivals include the International Firework Festival held in August in The Hague, and craft festivals and horse fairs in the other provinces.

INTERNET LINKS

www.holland.com/us/tourism/holland-information/kings-day-us.htm
The tourism board describes the celebration of King's Day.

www.telegraph.co.uk/gardening/gardeningpicturegalleries /9675142/Huge-floats-covered-in-flowers-at-the-Bloemencorso- Zundert-floral-parade.html
The *Telegraph*'s slideshow displays pictures from a recent Zundert Floral Parade.

www.timeanddate.com/holidays/netherlands
This website gives a listing of the holidays observed in the Netherlands.

FOOD

The Albert Cuypstraat Market in Amsterdam is known for its cheese, fish, spices, and vegetables.

13

THE DUTCH ARE KNOWN FOR STEWS, meats, and of course, pies, tarts, and cookies. These treats are enjoyed around the world—in 2015, the Vermont-based company Ben & Jerry's released a new ice cream flavor, Spectacular Speculoos, that includes pieces of Dutch cookies called *speculoos*. It's no surprise that Dutch cooking has inspired international trends. Cooking in the Netherlands often involves generous helpings of butter, cheese, and bread. According to *Conde Nast Traveler*, Dutch chefs have made the Netherlands "a culinary destination to watch."

Historically, the Dutch ate hearty meals in the face of cold, difficult winters. Traditional Dutch fare is high in fats and carbohydrates, though portions are smaller than those of the past.

VEGETABLES, MEAT, AND FISH

Winter or summer vegetables abound, and they are either grown in the fields or raised in the greenhouses that cover so much of South Holland. Dutch cooks can count on endless supplies of potatoes and curly kale, onions and carrots, spinach and peas, squash, several types of green and white beans, and a wide range of vegetables for salads. Less

Ontbijkoek is often served with butter.

common items, such as asparagus, fennel, artichokes, and eggplant, are also available. There are also plentiful supplies of fish, including salmon and trout, and seafood, such as lobster, shrimp, and scallops.

MEALS

Breakfast, called *ontbijt* (ont-BAYD), is a bread-and-butter affair in the Netherlands. The table is laden with several different kinds of bread and a variety of toppings—thin slices of smoked beef or other cold meats, sausages, tinned fish, preserves, and cheese. These are used to make open sandwiches with slices of bread— from plain white loaves, golden whole wheat, and heavy black rye bread, to tasty raisin and seed bread. Sometimes there may be croissants, crunchy dried bread, currant rolls, and *ontbijkoek* (ont-BAYD-kook)—a spiced bread flavored with dark brown sugar, molasses, ground cloves, cinnamon, ginger, and nutmeg.

Lunch is similar, although there may be a warm dish—perhaps a vegetable soup, an omelette, or the popular *uitsmijter* (OUTS-may-ter). This is an open sandwich of buttered bread generously topped with thinly sliced roast beef or ham, and crowned by two fried eggs. The name *uitsmijter* literally means "chucker out." It came about many years back when it was dreamed up as a farewell snack for the end of a party. A tasty and filling quick snack, it is served in lunch bars and cafés all over the Netherlands.

Lunch was formerly the main meal of the day, but with changing lifestyles and with more people working regular office hours, the Dutch now have their main meal early in the evening, at around 6 or 7 p.m. However, farmers who start work at dawn and others who find it more convenient to eat the main meal earlier still do so around midday. Throughout the day, people have several breaks for tea or coffee with a cookie or, as a special treat, a piece of cake or some chocolate.

TYPICAL FARE

The main meal of the day, be it lunch or dinner, often begins with a substantial vegetable soup. Occasionally, a thinner bouillon with meatballs or noodles is served. Other appetizers might be fresh grapefruit or a small, cold dish.

The main course includes fish or meat with vegetables. Potatoes are almost always served. The Dutch value the texture and flavor even of the plain, boiled potato and eat a lot of them with their main meal. They boil or steam potatoes with a small amount of water in a pan covered by a tightly fitting lid. When all the liquid has been absorbed, the potatoes are shaken in the pan until they are flaky and dry.

Surprisingly, uitsmijter is a lunch dish.

CHEESE!

Unlike Great Britain, where cheese is often eaten for dessert, cheese is an important part of breakfast and lunch in the Netherlands but seldom appears at the main meal.

The Dutch have been making cheese since before the Middle Ages, and with modern methods, the Netherlands is now one of Europe's leading cheesemakers.

Milk arriving in large tanker trucks at the cheese factory is held in vast stainless steel vats, where it is heated or pasteurized to kill harmful bacteria. The fat content of the milk is then reduced, sometimes by use of a centrifuge, depending on the type of cheese to be made. In the case of Gouda (HOW-dah) cheese, for example, the milk is skimmed to a fat content of 3.5 percent. The milk is then ready for making cheese, a process that is now controlled by computer.

The milk is transferred to a curd-making unit, in which the curd is separated from the fluid by coagulation. The whey (fluid) is sucked off and the remaining curd is pressed into molds. Finally, it is immersed in a brine bath for several days and then dried and packed. In a modern cheese factory, five thousand cheeses, each weighing about 25 pounds (11 kilograms), can be made daily.

Some cheeses are round; others are loaf-shaped. The best-known varieties outside the Netherlands are Gouda and Edam (AY-dam). Gouda is round like a cartwheel with bulging sides, and Edam cheese has a cannonball shape with a waxy red coating. This originated from the custom of dipping the cheeses intended for sale in a protective wax covering. Nowadays, the protective coating is often supplemented by a red cellophane wrapper.

Of the 550 million tons (495 million t) of cheese produced each year in the Netherlands, 98 percent comes from over fifty highly automated factories.

Mashed potatoes are prepared with milk, nutmeg, and butter or margarine, then beaten until they are white and creamy. Occasionally, they are dotted with butter and browned under the grill or in the oven. Potato salad is made with freshly boiled potatoes dressed with a mustard, onion, vinegar, and mayonnaise sauce, and garnished with chopped parsley. For something special, small pears poached in spiced red wine are a popular side dish.

Desserts tend to be fairly simple. They include fruit, ice cream, fruit pies, and bread-based puddings made with eggs and dried fruit. Pancakes are also popular and, like pies and puddings, are often served with cream.

SPECIALTY DISHES

Popular Dutch dishes include minced meatballs, beans and bacon, and chicken served with applesauce. Smoked sausage is used in *erwtensoep* (ERT-en-soop)—a thick winter soup made from peas—or in hashes of mashed potatoes and other vegetables.

The Dutch have many tasty stews. The simplest is a combination of beef, potatoes, onions, and carrots. There is also the rich Hunter's Dish, with layers of stewed venison, sliced potatoes, apples, and fried onions. Sometimes it is made into a kind of pie by omitting the potato slices and replacing them with a topping of mashed potato.

Another Dutch specialty is the pancake. These are usually the size of dinner plates—about 12 inches (30 cm) in diameter—and are made with yeast. They come in two varieties—dinner pancakes served with smoked sausage or bacon, and sweet ones topped with a rich syrup, apples and cream, or ice cream. A favorite dessert is a custard called *vla* (vlah) that comes in several fruit flavors, chocolate, and vanilla. For other desserts, there are waffles and *poffertjes* (POF-er-tches). Poffertjes are small, round doughnuts without a hole or a filling, sprinkled with confectioner's sugar.

Erwtensoep is just one of the Netherlands' popular stews.

BEVERAGES

When having a drink with Dutch people, it is customary to raise one's glass and wish them *Proost* (prost) or *Gezondheid* (heh-ZONT-hayt), meaning "Your health." This is the equivalent of saying "Cheers!"

The national drink, *jenever* (jeh-NAY-ver), comes in two varieties—*jonge* (yong, or young), which is almost colorless, and *oude* (owd, or old), which is pale yellow and stronger. Both are drunk undiluted and in small quantities. People who prefer a lighter drink have beer, wine, or fruit liqueurs such as apricot or cherry brandy.

When it comes to beer, which almost everyone drinks, the most popular variety is a light brew. Some Dutch beers, such as Heineken, are sold all over the world. Wine is sometimes drunk with meals. Common after-dinner drinks include a creamy eggnog called Advocaat or a bourbon.

SEASONAL FOODS

April is the time for plovers' eggs, young asparagus begins to appear in May, and the oyster and mussel season begins in July. Autumn and winter bring a demand for game, especially wild boar.

King Willem-Alexander (*right*) is presented with the first barrel of herring of the year in 2013.

At the start of the herring season each spring, fishing boats compete to bring back the first boatload of herring. By tradition, the first barrel of new herring is always presented to the king.

LOCAL SPECIALTIES

Different provinces also have special dishes. In the southern Catholic areas, fish is widely served and is often eaten on Fridays. A great deal of fish and seafood is also consumed in the coastal provinces. Further inland, and especially in the northern polders where cattle, pigs, and chickens are bred, meat is eaten in larger quantities.

Specific dishes are often associated with individual towns. The people of Arnhem, for instance, have a casserole similar to Hungarian goulash, while *vlaai*, also known as Limburg pies—a thin, flat pie filled with fruit—is named after the southernmost province. Another delightful dessert is The Hague Bluff. As residents of The Hague are often thought by other Dutch people to be showing off, the light and fluffy Hague Bluff—made from no more than fruit syrup, sugar, and an egg white—is associated with their elegant city.

The Hague Bluff is drizzled with a tart berry sauce.

QUICK BITES

Sometimes work and other conditions leave little time to prepare and eat food at home. This presents few problems for the Dutch, who can take their pick of cheap and tasty snacks from street stalls and cafés. If they feel like treating themselves to something exotic, then the Indonesian *rijsttafel* (RAYS-tah-fel, meaning rice table), fits the bill.

The ever-popular uitsmijter probably comes at the top of the list of quick snacks, but it is closely followed by numerous varieties of filled *broodjes* (BROH-tches), or soft bread rolls. These are the Netherlands' equivalent of an American sandwich. Sandwich fillings are almost the same as those for

Snack bars are a common sight throughout the Netherlands, but FEBO automats give hungry customers a unique way to purchase fast food. An automat is a wall of food options that are already prepared. Patrons insert their coins into a slot, just like a vending machine, and then open a tiny glass door to grab their selection. FEBO automats can be found throughout the Netherlands—there are over sixty locations! The highest concentration of FEBO locations is in Amsterdam, where there are twenty-two FEBO stores to choose from. At FEBO, patrons can grab cheeseburgers, French fries, milkshakes, and chicken wings, among other options.

J. I. de Borst started FEBO fifty-five years ago in Amsterdam. De Borst is still very involved with the day-to-day operations of the business. Originally a pastry chef, de Borst prides himself on the quality of the food at every FEBO location.

breakfast and lunch, but sometimes with more expensive items like steak tartare, shrimp, and spiced ground beef. In the bigger towns, plain rolls are sometimes replaced by stuffed croissants.

Other fast-food snacks include French fries with mayonnaise, and pancakes garnished with bacon or ham.

INDONESIAN FOOD

The Dutch tell a joke about one of their compatriots who complained that a restaurant had only fancy foreign food on the menu. He especially complained about the lack of good old Dutch fare like his favorite rijsttafel. This story illustrates the extent to which Indonesian food (such as this man's beloved rijsttafel) has been absorbed into the Netherlands.

The rijsttafel comprises a selection of spicy dishes served with steamed rice and accompanied by fiery *sambals* (SAHM-bahls), a strong chilli paste, and side dishes of hard-boiled eggs, shrimp, and other items. Many dishes are cooked in coconut milk, spiced with ground coriander, cumin, and yellow turmeric, and flavored with sesame oil or soy sauce. Other ingredients include pungent dried-shrimp paste and lemongrass.

A simple meal might have as few as half a dozen dishes, while a banquet could have sixteen and thirty dishes with a selection of meat and vegetable curries.

Beef *rendang* (REHN-dahng) is a favorite on most menus, together with *panggang* (PAHNG-gahng, or barbecued) pork, chicken, and fish served with mild to red-hot sauces. Vegetables can be cooked in coconut milk with curry spices or served as *gado gado* (gah-doh gah-doh), a salad with a peanut sauce. A similar peanut sauce accompanies *satay* (SAH-teh), grilled meat on skewers garnished with slices of cucumber and raw onion.

INTERNET LINKS

dutchfood.about.com/od/aboutdutchcooking/u/Traditional DutchFood.htm
An extensive resource for traditional Dutch foods, this website is divided into easy-to-search categories.

www.nytimes.com/1989/09/13/garden/a-food-historian-works-to-give-the-dutch-their-due.html
The *New York Times* explores the work of Peter G. Rose, translator of the Dutch cookbook *The Sensible Cook* in "A Food Historian Works To Give the Dutch Their Due."

www.thedutchtable.com
Recipes and cultural information are featured on the Dutch Table.

HONINGKOEK (DUTCH HONEY CAKE)

6 eggs
1 cup (201 g) sugar
1 cup (340 g) honey
2 tablespoons (30 mL) oil
3 ½ cups (448 g) sifted all-purpose flour
1 ½ teaspoons (6 g) baking powder
1 teaspoon (8 g) baking soda
1 teaspoon (4 g) cinnamon
1 teaspoon (4 g) cloves
1 teaspoon (4 g) allspice
½ cup (75 g) raisins
½ cup (65 g) walnuts

Preheat your oven to 325°F (163°C).

In a large bowl, whisk eggs, sugar and honey until the mixture is smooth.

Add the oil to the eggs, sugar, and honey.

In another bowl, sift the flour, baking powder, baking soda, cinnamon, cloves, and allspice.

Slowly fold the dry ingredients into the mixture of eggs, sugar, and honey.

Stir until the batter is completely mixed.

Add the raisins and walnuts.

Grease a 9 x 13 x 2 inch (23 x 33 x 5 cm) pan.

Pour the batter into the pan and bake for about 60 minutes or until the cake is golden and a toothpick comes out clean.

HUTSPOT (DUTCH HOTPOT)

7 medium-sized potatoes
6 large carrots
4 medium onions
1 cup (175 g) of ham
Cooking oil
Butter
Salt

Peel the potatoes and cut them into quarters.

Peel the carrots and slice into ½-inch (1.2-centimeter) rounds.

Dice the onions.

Cube the ham.

Add the cooking oil to a pan and cook the potatoes until soft.

In another pan, cook the carrots, onions, and ham with a pinch of salt until the carrots are soft.

Use a slotted spoon to separate the vegetables and ham from the liquid.

Combine the vegetables and ham to the potatoes and mash.

Add the juices from the vegetable and ham mixture and butter to taste.

Serve with sausage.

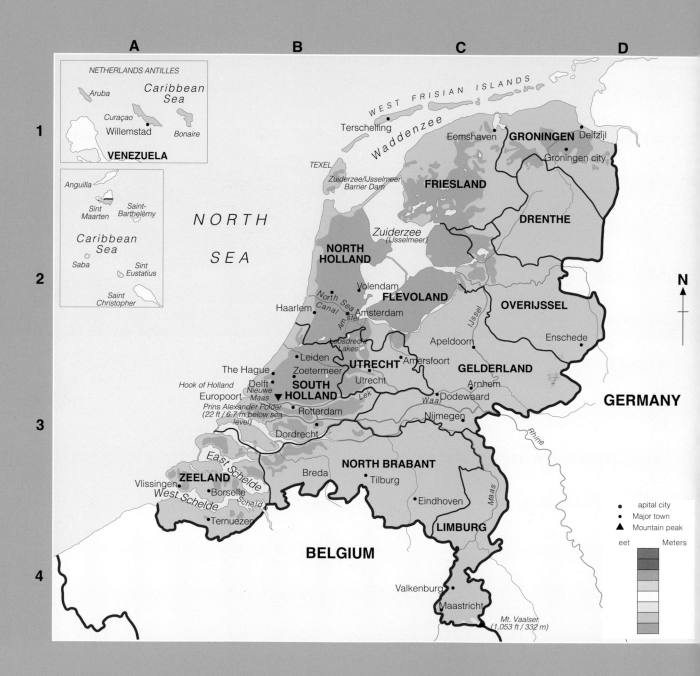

A **B** **C** **D**

NETHERLANDS ANTILLES

Caribbean Sea

Aruba

Curaçao
Willemstad

Bonaire

VENEZUELA

1

Anguilla

Sint Maarten

Saint-Barthelèmy

Caribbean Sea

Saba

Sint Eustatius

Saint Christopher

2

N O R T H

S E A

WEST FRISIAN ISLANDS

Terschelling

Waddenzee

Eemshaven

GRONINGEN

Delfzijl

Groningen city

TEXEL

Zuiderzee/IJsselmeer Barrier Dam

FRIESLAND

DRENTHE

Zuiderzee (IJsselmeer)

NORTH HOLLAND

Volendam

FLEVOLAND

OVERIJSSEL

North Sea Canal

Haarlem

Amsterdam

Enschede

Amstel

Loosdrecht Lakes

Leiden

Apeldoorn

Amersfoort

GELDERLAND

The Hague

Zoetermeer

UTRECHT

Hook of Holland

Delft

Nieuwe Maas

SOUTH HOLLAND

Utrecht

Arnhem

Europoort

Lek

Dodewaard

Prins Alexander Polder (22 ft / 6.7 m below sea level)

Rotterdam

Waal

Nijmegen

3

Dordrecht

Rhine

East Schelde

ZEELAND

NORTH BRABANT

Vlissingen

Borselle

Breda

Tilburg

West Schelde

Schelde

Eindhoven

Maas

Ternuezen

LIMBURG

BELGIUM

N

GERMANY

4

Valkenburg

Maastricht

Mt. Vaalser (1,053 ft / 332 m)

● capital city

• Major town

▲ Mountain peak

eet   Meters

MAP OF NETHERLANDS

ECONOMIC NETHERLANDS

Agriculture

🐄 Dairy Products

🌷 Flowers

Manufacturing

🏭 Industrial Complex

💎 Diamond Cutting

Services

🚢 Port

ABOUT THE ECONOMY

OVERVIEW

The Netherlands is a highly industrialized nation. Trade based on the transit of goods accounts for more than half the country's income. The Netherlands is the second-largest exporter of agricultural goods in the world, and the third-largest exporter of dairy products.

GROSS DOMESTIC PRODUCT (GDP)

US $869.5 billion (2014)

GDP BY SECTOR

Agriculture 2 percent, industry 21.4 percent, services 76.6 percent (2014)

AREA

Total: 16,033 square miles
(41,526 sq km)
Land: 13,082 square miles
(33,883 sq km)
Water: 2,951 square miles
(7,643 sq km)

LAND USE

Arable 31 percent, permanent crops 1 percent, forest 11 percent

CURRENCY

1 euro (EUR) = 100 cents
Notes: 5, 10, 20, 50, 100, 200, 500 euros
Coins: 1, 2, 5, 10, 20, 50 cents; 1, 2 euros
USD 1 = EUR 0.88 (October 2015)

AGRICULTURAL PRODUCTS

Sugar beets, fruit, vegetables, flowers, potatoes, grains, livestock

NATURAL RESOURCES

Petroleum, natural gas, arable land

POPULATION

16,947,904 (July 2015)

WORKFORCE

8,998,325 (2013)

WORKFORCE BY SECTOR

Agriculture 1.8 percent, industry 17 percent, services 81.2 percent (2013)

UNEMPLOYMENT RATE

7.4 percent (2014)

PORTS AND HARBORS

Amsterdam, Delfzijl, Dordrecht, Eemshaven, Groningen, Haarlem, IJmuiden, Maastricht, Rotterdam, Terneuzen, Utrecht, Vlissingen

MAJOR EXPORTS

Machinery, transportation equipment, food, chemicals, flowers, electrical equipment

MAJOR TRADE PARTNERS

Germany, Belgium, United Kingdom, France, United States, Italy, China

MAJOR IMPORTS

Clothing, foods, chemicals, fuels, machinery, transportation equipment

CULTURAL NETHERLANDS

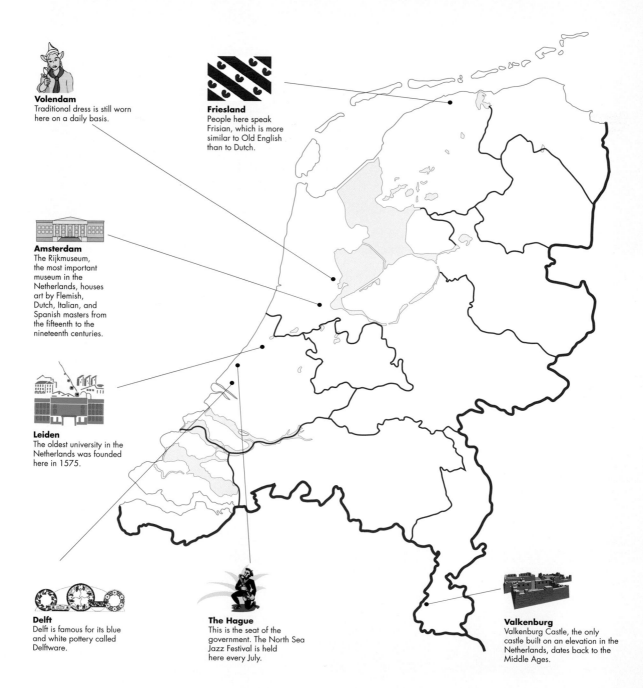

Volendam
Traditional dress is still worn here on a daily basis.

Friesland
People here speak Frisian, which is more similar to Old English than to Dutch.

Amsterdam
The Rijkmuseum, the most important museum in the Netherlands, houses art by Flemish, Dutch, Italian, and Spanish masters from the fifteenth to the nineteenth centuries.

Leiden
The oldest university in the Netherlands was founded here in 1575.

Delft
Delft is famous for its blue and white pottery called Delftware.

The Hague
This is the seat of the government. The North Sea Jazz Festival is held here every July.

Valkenburg
Valkenburg Castle, the only castle built on an elevation in the Netherlands, dates back to the Middle Ages.

ABOUT THE CULTURE

COUNTRY NAME
Kingdom of the Netherlands

CAPITAL
Amsterdam

FLAG DESCRIPTION
Three equal horizontal bands of red, white, and blue.

LANGUAGES
Dutch. There are also several dialects, named after the regions in which they are spoken. Frisian is a separate language, spoken in the province of Friesland and not understood by ordinary Dutch speakers.

ETHNIC GROUPS
Dutch descent 81 percent, non-Western descent 10 percent, other 9 percent

LIFE EXPECTANCY
Men 79 years (2015), women 83 years (2015)

LITERACY RATE
99 percent (2015)

RELIGIONS
Christianity 45 percent; no religion 46 percent; Islam 4 percent; Hinduism, Judaism, and Buddhism 6 percent

EDUCATION
Full-time school is compulsory from ages five to sixteen and paid for by the government. Most schools are coeducational.

LEADERS IN POLITICS
Prince William of Orange, Queen Beatrix (1980—2013), King Willem-Alexander (2013—present), Queen Maxima (2013—present), Jan Peter Balkenende (prime minister, 2002—2010), Mark Rutte (prime minister, 2010—present)

IMPORTANT LITERARY FIGURES
Erasmus (translated the New Testament from Greek to Latin), Gerbrand Adriaensz Bredero (poet and playwright during the Dutch Golden Age), Joost van den Vondel (dramatist and national poet in the seventeenth century), Harry Mulisch (twentieth-century writer), Anne Frank (Dutch Jewish diarist, victim of Nazi persecution)

IMPORTANT SCHOLARS
Thomas à Kempis (religious author), Hugo Grotius (author in international law, theologian, statesman, and poet), Baruch Spinoza (philosopher)

IMPORTANT ARTISTS
Rembrandt van Rijn, Vincent van Gogh, Jan Vermeer, Jan Steen, Frans Hals, Piet Mondrian, Hieronymus Bosch, Pieter Bruegel the Elder

TIMELINE

IN THE NETHERLANDS	IN THE WORLD
	753 BCE Rome is founded.
100 CE The Frisians, a Teutonic tribe, settle in what is now the Netherlands.	**116–117 CE** The Roman Empire reaches its greatest extent.
800 CE Frisians accept Christianity from the Franks, a conglomeration of German tribes.	**1000** The Chinese perfect gunpowder and begin to use it in warfare.
1489–1490 The Netherlands is ravaged by the plague.	**1530** Beginning of transatlantic slave trade organized by the Portuguese in Africa.
	1558–1603 Reign of Elizabeth I of England.
1568–1648 The Eighty Years' War eventually results in the Netherlands' freedom from Spanish rule.	
1626 Dutch explorer Peter Minuit takes over the island of Manhattan, and the southern part of the island is named Nieuw Amsterdam.	
1600–1700s The Dutch colonize what is now Indonesia, naming it the Dutch East Indies.	**1776** US Declaration of Independence signed.
	1789–1799 The French Revolution.
	1861 The US Civil War begins.
	1869 The Suez Canal is opened.
1914–1918 The Dutch do not participate in World War I.	**1914** World War I begins.
1939 The Dutch make a declaration that they will not take sides in World War II.	**1939** World War II begins.
1940–1945 The Nazis occupy the Netherlands.	
1945 The Netherlands is a founding member of the United Nations.	**1945** The United States drops atomic bombs on Hiroshima and Nagasaki.

IN THE NETHERLANDS	IN THE WORLD
1949 The Dutch East Indies declares independence and becomes Indonesia.	**1949** The North Atlantic Treaty Organization (NATO) is formed.
	1957 The Russians launch *Sputnik 1*.
	1966–1969 The Chinese Cultural Revolution.
1980 Queen Beatrix succeeds Queen Juliana as queen of the Netherlands.	**1986** Nuclear power disaster at Chernobyl in Ukraine.
	1991 Breakup of the Soviet Union.
2000 The Netherlands declares euthanasia legal.	**1997** Hong Kong is returned to China.
2001 Same-sex couples are allowed to get married and adopt children.	**2001** Terrorists crash planes in New York, Washington, DC, and Pennsylvania.
2002 The euro becomes Dutch currency; Jan Peter Balkenende becomes the prime minister.	**2003** War in Iraq.
	2005 London hit by terrorist bombings.
	2008 Barack Obama elected US president.
2010 Mark Rutte becomes Prime Minister.	**2010** Massive earthquakes devastate Haiti and Chile.
2013 Queen Beatrix abdicates. Her son Willem-Alexander becomes king.	**2011** "Arab Spring" movement topples governments in the Middle East.
2014 196 Dutch nationals die aboard Malaysia Airlines flight MH17, stoking tensions with Russia.	**2014** ISIS terrorists take over large parts of Syria and Iraq.

GLOSSARY

abdication
The act of stepping down from the throne.

Algemeen Beschaafd Nederlands
(AHL-heh-main Behs-SHAAHFT NAY-der-lands)
The standard Dutch language that is used for official purposes and is taught in schools.

dike
A levee or river bank built of earth, used to control flooding of rivers or the sea.

Europoort (YEW-ROH-port)
A complex of docks, berths, warehouses, and basins that line the mouth of the Niewe Maas river from Rotterdam to the North Sea. It ranks among the world's largest port complexes.

Eurosystem
The "monetary authority" of the European Union that oversees the Euro.

formateur (form-a-TERH)
The Dutch prime minister, who forms the government.

gezellig (gheh-ZEL-lig)
A cozy, warm atmosphere in Dutch homes.

hofjes (HOFF-yehs)
Homes for senior citizens.

Holland
The name of two of the provinces in the Netherlands (North Holland and South Holland); these provinces were historically trading sites, which led traders to call the whole nation Holland.

inauguration
A ceremony that marks the beginning of a public official's time in office.

klompen (KLOM-pen)
Dutch clogs, still commonly worn when doing heavy or dirty work.

Mevrouw (mehv-FRAOW)
Misses.

Mijnheer (mehn-NEER)
Mister.

ontbijt (ont-BAYD)
Breakfast, which is usually a meal of bread and various toppings.

polder (POHL-der)
An area of low-lying land that has been reclaimed from the sea or other body of water.

rijsttafel (RAYS-tah-fel)
An Indonesian buffet-type meal where rice is served with many other dishes of meat, fish, and vegetables.

States General
The Dutch parliament, comprising the Upper and Lower House.

verzuilen (ver-ZUEH-len)
The pillarization system, where people and society are distinguished by the different systems of beliefs, or pillars, to which they belong.

voetbal (VOOT-bahl)
Soccer, the most popular sport in the Netherlands.

FOR FURTHER INFORMATION

BOOKS

Besamusca, Emmeline, and Jaap Verheul, eds. *Discovering the Dutch: On Culture and Society of the Netherlands*. Amsterdam: Amsterdam University Press, 2015.

Janin, Hunt, and Ria Van Eil. *CultureShock! Netherlands: A Survival Guide to Customs and Etiquette*. Tarrytown, New York: Marshall Cavendish, 2012.

Steves, Rick and Gene Openshaw. *Rick Steves Amsterdam and the Netherlands*. Berkeley, CA: Avalon Travel Publishing, 2015.

Wielenga, Friso. *A History of the Netherlands: From the Sixteenth Century to the Present Day*. Translated by Lynne Richards. New York: Bloomsbury Academic, 2015.

WEBSITES

CIA World Factbook. https://www.cia.gov/library/publications/the-world-factbook/geos/nl.html

Dutch News. http://www.dutchnews.nl

The Dutch Royal Family. http://www.holland.com/us/tourism/holland-information/the-dutch-royal-family.htm

Embassy of the Kingdom of the Netherlands in Washington, DC, USA. http://www.the-netherlands.org

Statistics Netherlands. http://www.cbs.nl/en-GB/menu/home/default.htm

MUSIC

Dutch Delight: Organ Music from the Golden Age, Brilliant Classics, 2015.

Dutch Folk Songs, Folkways Records, 2012.

Het regende zon by Ellen ten Damme, CNR Music, 2012.

BIBLIOGRAPHY

BBC News, Netherlands Timeline
   http://www.bbc.co.uk/news/world-europe-17741525
CBS, Statistics Netherlands
   http://www.cbs.nl/en-GB/menu/home/default.htm
CIA World Fact Book, Europe: Netherlands
   https://www.cia.gov/library/publications/the-world-factbook/geos/nl.html
Guardian, Netherlands Holidays + Festivals
   http://www.theguardian.com/travel/netherlands+festivals
Government of the Netherlands
   https://www.government.nl/
Holland.com, Tourism in Holland
   http://www.holland.com/us/tourism.htm
UNdata, Netherlands
   http://data.un.org/CountryProfile.aspx?crName=NETHERLANDS
US Department of State, Netherlands Fact Sheet
   http://www.state.gov/r/pa/ei/bgn/3204.htm
Waterfield, Bruno. "Dutch Crowning: King Willem-Alexander Becomes Europe's Youngest Monarch." Telegraph. April 30, 2013
   http://www.telegraph.co.uk/news/worldnews/europe/netherlands/10027014/Dutch-crowning-King-Willem-Alexander-becomes-Europes-youngest-monarch.html
The World Bank, Data | Netherlands
   http://data.worldbank.org/country/netherlands

INDEX

INDEX